I am thrilled to read **More Great New**_____ _____ Lameiro
has been consistent and outstanding in his predictive analysis of
the American political landscape and has been on target in
predicting election results with far greater accuracy than the
traditional polling services. He has appeared weekly on my
nationally syndicated talk program and has been an outstanding
contributor for my audience. Enjoy the book. It will be a landmark
in defining this nation's political future.

> Mike Siegel, Ph.D., J.D.
> Nationally Syndicated, Talk Radio Show Host
> The Mike Siegel Show

Dr. Gerard F. Lameiro has written a masterful guide to America's
bright future. The man who correctly predicted the Trump
revolution and exact election results now offers **More Great News
for America**. No gloom and doom here, just the facts, as Dr.
Lameiro has his finger on the pulse of America. Our best days are
yet to come and the "Nostradamus of Political Elections" spells out
a future within our grasp. You'll discover how the "good guys"
succeed as a conservative tide of prosperity and a renewed America
returns.

> Erskine
> Nationally Syndicated, Talk Radio Show Host
> Erskine Overnight Show

A true visionary and one of America's top political analysts, Dr.
Gerard Lameiro, has a long track record of accurately predicting
election outcomes and forecasting major change on the national
scene. He has done it once again. His latest book **More Great
News for America** will inspire you and give you a unique look at
the bright days looming in our nation's future. Prescient. Hopeful.
A must read!

> Drew Mariani
> Nationally Syndicated, Talk Radio Show Host
> Award-winning Writer, Producer and Director
> The Drew Mariani Show

Gerard has always had his index finger on America's pulse. He always has believed in our greatness and provides the heartbeat of Trump's great success ...

Bill Cunningham
Nationally Syndicated, Talk Radio Show Host
Live on Sunday Night, It's Bill Cunningham Show

Dr. Gerard Lameiro is a refreshingly objective cultural and political analyst and prognosticator at a time when so many in the media are running to insert their slanted, subjective opinions as news and fact. It is why my audience loves it when he is scheduled to be on the Prime Time radio show. His information and compelling delivery are second to none.

Dan Klein
Talk Radio Host
Prime Time with Dan Klein Show

Dr. Lameiro sets the gold standard for other political analysts. While they appear to be reading "tea leaves," Dr. Lameiro issues fact-based predictions which become reality. Others pontificate and confuse, but Dr. Lameiro is conversational, clear, to the point and my audience can't get enough of him.

Larry Conners
Talk Radio Host
Larry Conners USA

I have interviewed over 10,000 guests in the course of my career as a radio talk show host, most of whom have PhDs. Without a doubt, Dr. Lameiro is one of America's most prescient, compelling and uplifting scholars. He doesn't just explain what has happened or what is going to happen, he explains the whys and wherefores! Dr. Lameiro understands what Americans want and need from their political leaders by way of analyzing data in a manner that is simply beyond the capabilities of most prognosticators and pundits.

Andy Caldwell
Talk Radio Host
The Andy Caldwell Radio Show

I have had the pleasure of having Dr. Gerard Lameiro on my show, Drive Time Live, many times over the past couple of years talking about his book **Great News for America**. Forget all the polls, his insight and predictions into political trends are spot-on. I'm ready for **More Great News for America**!

Mark Hahn
Talk Radio Host
Drive Time Live with Mark Hahn Show

Everything you wanted to know about polls and the political parties they track, but were afraid to ask.

David Horowitz
Author
Big Agenda: President Trump's Plan to Save America

Dr. Lameiro has become one of the most trusted voices in conservative commentary today. His predictions concerning the 2016 presidential election were spot on. The new book **More Great News For America** offers even more insights into our country's political climate and a reliable roadmap for the upcoming elections.

Perry Atkinson
President & CEO, theDove Media Inc.
TV and Talk Radio Show Host
Focus Today Show

You'll want to dig deep into Dr. Lameiro's new book. He has both an uncanny ability to accurately predict the election and is brilliant in his analysis. I may not always like his predictions, but there's no getting around his educated genius!"

Ethan Bearman
Talk Radio Show Host
Ethan Bearman Show

More
Great News for
America

The Dawning of the New Conservative Era
(How and Why the Good Guys Win in the End!)

Gerard Lameiro, Ph.D.

Author of *Great News for America*
"Nostradamus of Political Elections"

For more information on the author, or his other books, or his
weekly blog posts, or additional information,
please visit GreatNewsForAmerica.com.

Book cover design and layout by MDW Graphics & Type,
mdwgraphics.com.

First Edition.

Printed by CreateSpace, An Amazon.com Company.

Available from Amazon.com, CreateSpace.com, and
other retail outlets.

Available on Kindle and other devices.

To Lauri

Table of Contents

Part II – What Will Happen to American Political Parties in the Coming Years?

Part III – What Will Happen with America's Top Political Issues in the Future?

Part IV – What Will Happen in the Upcoming Elections and in the Future?

Preface

The optimistic vision and positive message of my fourth book, *Great News for America,* struck a chord in the hearts, souls, and minds of countless Americans across our nation before, during, and after the historic and critical presidential election of 2016. During 2016, I was interviewed on 469 TV and Talk Radio programs mostly across America and a few around the world. Those interviews led to a considerable amount of feedback that made me conclude people were genuinely moved by my optimistic vision for America.

Within that book, *Great News for America,* I made ten bold and powerful predictions that have largely come true by most accounts. I consider at least nine of the ten predictions to have come true or to be still in the process of coming true. Some people credit me with being ten for ten on those predictions.

My long-range models that run 24 – 36 years in length for assessing and predicting historic and critical presidential elections, along with their corresponding American Constitutional Eras, seem to have been vindicated, along with my short-range models that look at periods from 2 – 8 years, as well as my dynamic election models that track variables covering a more immediate timeframe of 1 – 24 months prior to Election Day itself.

Along with the ten predictions I made in *Great News for America,* I separately and accurately predicted a Trump victory long before most pollsters and pundits gave Trump even a small chance of winning the presidential election. In my state-by-state Electoral College forecast, I also correctly predicted every state that candidate Trump actually carried in the 2016 election, including the crucial states of Pennsylvania, Michigan, and Wisconsin. Of course, my forecasts flew in the face of conventional wisdom at that time, as well as the many polls that showed Clinton leading and the likely winner of the election.

More Great News for America builds on the optimistic vision and positive message of *Great News for America*. It updates where America stands using both my long-range presidential election and American Constitutional Era models and by my short-range electoral models. It includes my latest dynamic election models as well. This book avoids the jargon of specialists and the nitty-gritty of mathematicians and statisticians, preferring to speak in straight-forward language to the author's readers and also to the author's TV and Talk Radio show listeners. No math or statistics are needed to read this book.

More Great News for America goes on to make new predictions, many bold and powerful, related to the political parties and their viability, the actual upcoming Congressional elections, the makeup of the new House and Senate, and achieving or not achieving the Trump agenda in the future. It also looks ahead to the upcoming presidential election.

This book clearly explains how and why the good guys win in the end. The good guys are the American people.

Why am I writing this book? As with *Great News for America*, I have a heartfelt reason for writing this book. In fact, I'm writing this book from my heart to the hearts of all Americans. *More Great News for America* represents my understanding of American History, my analysis of the present politics we are witnessing every day in America, and my vision for America's optimistic future. My vision for America continues to include morality and freedom as well as peace and prosperity, for all Americans.

I still believe that we have a great future ahead of us in America.

Why do we have a great future ahead of us? America's great future is built on a rock solid foundation. America's truth was established on our Judeo-Christian heritage. It began with our Founding Fathers and our founding documents. It lives on today in the Declaration of Independence that provides us with our moral principles, and in the Constitution that provides us with our political principles, and also guarantees all of our liberties.

America's truth began with the exceptional idea that God is the

"Author of our Liberty" and that liberty was given by God to all the people, and then was loaned by the people to its elected representatives for limited purposes, for a limited time, when the representatives served the people faithfully and morally. In stark contrast across time and geography, the leaders of non-exceptional nations reigned more or less supreme over their subjects, and grudgingly gave limited freedoms, for limited purposes, for limited times, to their subjects.

American Exceptionalism has never been the norm around the world.

America's truth continues on throughout all of the nation's moral and political challenges, all of the nation's wars and strife, and all of the nation's economic crises and hardships that this nation has met with valor, endured with courage, and overcome with fortitude and hard work in its 240-year plus history.

America is at a critical crossroads today. It has elected a strong, popular, and conservative president in the historic and critical presidential election of 2016. Yet, President Trump is facing unprecedented opposition from the Democratic Party, whose primary activity seems to be resistance to President Trump's mandate and agenda, as well as to the will of the American people.

In addition, President Trump faces considerable pushback and struggles from the ranks of the Establishment Republican Party that probably would have preferred one of their own to be nominated and elected president. If that were not enough, the president faces an unrelenting, negative old mainstream media that sometimes seems to report fake news as easily as it should report real news.

For quite a few years, Americans have been morally outraged because they believe America has gone off track. Americans continue to sense a growing and grave moral and political crisis. Sometimes, it's called a cultural war. Certainly, it represents a real cultural divide and often a cultural crisis. On the positive side, since the historic 2016 presidential election, Americans believe the economic malaise of the past ten years is rapidly coming to a close.

Economic optimism indexes are exceptionally strong and upbeat.

But, nevertheless, Americans are still concerned that our nation might not survive, or might not survive as a free nation. Americans worry that we are losing our religious freedom, political freedom, and economic freedom. They are deeply troubled by the fact that their representatives in the House and their senators are not honoring many of the promises made to constituents.

Americans sense that this crisis stems from politicians and others who have abandoned America's founding documents; who have foregone morality and freedom; who have overseen cronyism, corruption, and the intoxication of power; and who are quite literally ruining and destroying the greatest nation ever to exist on this planet. They are justifiably and deeply concerned for America.

My answer to those who think America's greatest days are over and my answer to those who think America's days as a free nation are over, is simple and direct. NO WAY.

The American people will not let this happen. The American people have been taking action in recent elections to right the ship of State. The American people will continue to take action in voting booths across the nation to realign political parties and political institutions as they see fit to reestablish morality and freedom. They have done so repeatedly in our 240-year plus history. They will do so again in the near future and beyond. That's why my vision for America is filled with enthusiasm, optimism, and energy.

Indeed, America will survive and America will remain free. America will continue to be the greatest, most creative, most innovative, most productive, and most generous nation in the history of the world. It will provide the greatest opportunities for its citizens, and it will provide the best future imaginable for its children and grandchildren. American Exceptionalism is alive and well, and it will continue to thrive as we move forward in the 21st century and beyond.

Who threatens America's morality and freedom, peace and prosperity? It's true, America has been under assault. America's morality and freedom, its peace and prosperity have all been threatened in recent years. Americans have experienced many related fears and anxieties.

It is worth noting why Americans have felt threatened as we approach the upcoming Congressional elections. We can place blame on what I call simply the "ISMs of Failure." The "ISMs of Failure" are: progressive socialism, democratic socialism, socialism, Marxism, communism, and anarchism. In a nutshell, these "ISMs of Failure" preach their own gospel of secular atheism and agnosticism (two more ISMs) that avoid morality and traditional family values, and work against religious freedom, political freedom, and economic freedom. They prefer to substitute the capricious Rule of Man for the solid Rule of Law. They prefer centralized authoritative government rather than our Constitution and freedom for all individuals.

One purpose of my writings and interviews on TV and Talk Radio is to refresh all of our collective memories about the fundamental goodness, integrity, and strength of America and its founding moral and political principles, as well as to help people see clearly through the fog of our current, grave national moral, cultural, and political challenges.

Regrettably, most Americans believe our government is still too corrupt, our system is not responsive to the voters, and we are still substantially off track. There are valid reasons for these enormous concerns, and more importantly, there are powerful conservative core principles we can follow, and there are common sense solutions we can achieve to the large issues we face. (For readers that want to delve into both the principles and the solutions to those issues, I recommend reading my previous book, *Great News for America*.)[1]

Americans resonate with the same moral theme that surfaced during the 2016 presidential campaign, "drain the swamp." Americans want to eliminate any corruption in Washington.

More Great News for America presents new solutions to our

political issues and new hope for considerable optimism for the future. After reading this book, you might even get a boost of enthusiasm, optimism, and energy. I hope so.

In truth and confidence, I envision a refreshed and reinvigorated America whose founding documents are once again revered, respected, adhered to, and followed closely. This morally renewed nation based on freedom, peace, and prosperity will be restored over a period of elections, including the upcoming Congressional elections.

Along with that renewal of the American spirit will come the continued dawning of the newest American Constitutional Era, the Conservative Era. (Again, for readers that want to delve into the various preceding American Constitutional Eras and the new Conservative Era that began in 2016, I recommend reading my previous book, *Great News for America*.)[2]

Progressive socialism, democratic socialism, socialism, Marxism, communism, and anarchism are the political models of failure in today's struggling world. They are the modern day soft and hard tyrannies that oppress individuals and stagnate or eliminate economic growth. They also lead to anger, division, and violence among people, and anger, violence, and war among nations.

Progressive socialism, democratic socialism, socialism, Marxism, communism, and anarchism all lack a framework for true morality and freedom. All fail spiritually, morally, culturally, politically, and economically. All bring pain and suffering to mankind. All lead to moral and economic bankruptcy.

In the long run, only through force and/or deception can they hold on to power. The question for these political models of failure, these "ISMs of Failure," is how long before they deplete the wealth of a nation, and how long before they cause a nation to slide into bankruptcy. There is no other answer because they only consume wealth created in the private sector, and never produce wealth in the public sector. They also produce moral bankruptcy and corruption in the process.

If someone wants to see an example of socialism's failure, consider the plight of Venezuela.

Proponents of socialism frequently overlook the obvious failures of socialism with the excuse that a particular country didn't implement their version of socialism correctly.

Let me emphasize one point now. All versions and all variations of socialism lead to moral and economic bankruptcy. The particular implementation of socialism is never the problem. It's the theory and the ideology of socialism that are doomed to failure from the outset.

Freedom works. Socialism fails.

While these political models of failure often make grandiose promises to those who succumb to their modern day forms of deception, corruption, and tyranny, they always fail to deliver on these same lofty promises.

Many have been seduced by the deception of the "ISMs of Failure." Many have succumbed to their unrealistic promises and their unending lies. Even those who are Christian often have been subtly seduced by socialism's offer to help the poor, neglecting the fact that their method robs their supposed beneficiaries of dignity and self-worth, while forcing them into a life of utter dependency and hopelessness, existing on the whims of big government. Socialism will give the crumbs of aid to keep citizens permanently dependent, but never the food of substance to allow citizens to become free, and independent, and prosperous.

The morality and freedom our Founding Fathers built on the eastern shores of America in the late 1700's offers us the antithesis of the "ISMs of Failure." American Exceptionalism is the path to civilizational success, to morality and freedom, and to peace and prosperity.

Freedom – religious freedom, political freedom, economic freedom – will always lead to spiritual and material growth. The "ISMs of Failure" always lead to moral and economic bankruptcy.

America's Future is Bright. My vision for America is optimistic and bright. As you read *More Great News for America,* you will see that America's future is indeed optimistic and positive.

Enjoy the book I have written from my heart to your heart. Enjoy America's bright future!

Remember that the good guys win in the end!

Introduction

There is truly more great news for America coming soon. Our optimism as a nation is high and growing even higher. Our economy is booming. GDP is up and growing stronger. The energy sector is up and to the right. Unemployment is low and the number of Americans working is high. The stock market is hitting one record high after another. Many have seen their 401Ks and IRAs jump up since President Trump's election.

Literally, trillions of dollars of new wealth have been created in America since President Trump was elected. Billions of new dollars are being invested in the American economy.

In foreign policy, we have America once again in a position of leadership on the world stage. We are leading from out front and no longer from behind. ISIS has been essentially defeated and North Korea's nuclear and ICBM ambitions have been largely contained. America has a new tough and powerful National Security Strategy.[3]

We are witnessing the dawning of the new Conservative Era in American Constitutional History with a conservative super-majority on the Supreme Court on the horizon in President Trump's first term of office. Indeed, President Trump will probably appoint three more Constitutional conservative justices to the Supreme Court in the next few years.

At the same time, we are seeing a related new Conservative Enlightenment that will impact America in positive ways for decades to come. Indeed, it is challenging to imagine all the wonderful developments that this Conservative Enlightenment will add to our lives and our lifestyles in the future. But, it will be amazing and spectacular.

Medical, technological, economic, educational, and recreational innovations and improvements will usher in a new quality of life for all Americans. Our lifestyles will stagger the imagination.

But, don't expect to read about all this great news in the old mainstream media. They are too busy attacking President Trump and resisting America's progress.

Why this news will not show up in the old mainstream media? Of course, you won't hear this news from the old mainstream media whose relentless attacks on America's traditional institutions and whose frequent fake news stories don't permit great news from being reported. True stories that don't fit the old mainstream media's socialist narratives are routinely rejected and go largely unreported.

Freedom is optimistic and positive. Socialism is pessimistic and negative.

Note that I use the term **old mainstream media** as opposed to **mainstream media** to highlight some important facts. First, the old mainstream media we have seen for the last few decades (ABC, CBS, NBC, *The New York Times, The Washington Post, Time, Newsweek,* etc.) is no longer "main stream." The old mainstream media has fallen out of touch with its customers who still seek truth and reality in their news reporting and who reject politically correct and ideologically-driven fake news stories. To illustrate, the infamous and inaccurate narrative "hands up, don't shoot" used after the Ferguson, Missouri shooting incident was ultimately discredited by the facts and was clearly false.[4]

Second, as our nation transitions into a new American Constitutional Era, again what I call the Conservative Era, a new mainstream media emerges in parallel.[5] Recall from my book *Great News for America* that with a new American Constitutional Era often comes a new mainstream media.[6]

The new mainstream media in the Conservative Era consists of the various new media, social media, and Talk Radio. This is a hugely significant trend for Americans and how they obtain their news.

We can see this trend take place in front of our eyes as the old mainstream media experiences revenue shortfalls, as their long-standing business models break, as they require staff layoffs, and as their businesses are significantly downsized. With their credibility falling, viewers, listeners, and readers drop by the wayside, seeking instead other news sources for truth and reality. The old mainstream media seems to have forgotten that the news industry, like any other industry, is there to serve customers, in this case, citizens who seek news, not made up socialist narratives.

At the same time, we witness the first American president ever to communicate consistently to the American people using tweets. While attacked by the old political and media establishment elites for his tweets, it makes sense to expect President Trump and future presidents to use our new mainstream media platforms versus relying on the tools of the past.

Moving forward in this overview, how do polls, models, trends, predictions, and forecasts really work in a presidential election? It might not be obvious at first glance. But, it should become clear as you read Part I in this book.

Why were the 2016 presidential election polls "wrong" about Clinton? Why were the Lameiro presidential election models right about Trump? I have gotten these questions many times and I answer them in this book.

In 2016, the polls generally indicated that Clinton would become our next president. I was somewhat amused by the political pundit in late October 2016 that stated on-air that there was no point for Clinton even attending the third presidential debate in Las Vegas because she was so far ahead in the polls that she essentially had won the election already.

Of course, my forecast was in sharp contrast to most polls in October 2016. In fact, I had clearly, consistently, and importantly, accurately predicted Trump's victory months earlier.

Part I of this book explains the differences between, and the relationship among polls, models, trends, predictions, and forecasts without boring readers with any complex mathematical and statistical details. It answers the compelling questions why the polls were so wrong and misleading in the 2016 presidential election, and why my models, trends, predictions, and forecasts were so accurate. Fortunately for readers, the answers are plain and simple and don't require rocket science to explain or to understand.

What will happen to American political parties in the next few years? If you think 2016 was an historic and critical presidential election that was characterized by a lot of startling events, you haven't seen anything yet. Major changes to political parties are likely to occur in the next few years. Some of these changes will probably shock you because they might seem totally unexpected today.

All of these changes however were actually set in motion by the 2016 presidential election and the underlying long-range, short-range, and dynamic election trends that I use in my forecasts. But, they have yet to fully play out.

Recall too from my previous book *Great News for America* that historic and critical presidential elections ultimately result in political party realignments.[7] It's happening now and it will dramatically lurch forward in the next few years.

Part II of this book leads you through stunning potential Democratic Party political realignments and answers questions such as:

- Will the Democratic Party even survive in the future?
- Will it be a minority party for a generation?
- Will it rename and rebrand itself to be the Progressive Socialist Party?
- Will it join forces with the old mainstream media to form the Globalist Party?
- Will it merge with the Green Party and the Socialist Party USA to form the Democratic Socialist Party?
- Will the Democratic Party simply shut down like the Whig Party?
- Will the Democratic Party ever elect another president?

Part II also addresses the following questions about the Republican Party:

- Who will win the battle for control of the Republican Party?
- Will it pass more conservative legislation?
- Will it be forced to become more conservative by voters?
- Will it morph into a new majority party – the Conservative Party?
- Will it split into two new parties – the Conservative Party and the Republican Progressive Party?
- Will the Republican Party or the Conservative Party become the majority party for a generation?

Expect incredible political party changes in the next few years.

What will happen with America's top political issues in the future? Besides dealing with the above major questions regarding the future of the political parties in America, this book goes on in Part III to discuss such political issues and questions as:

- Will America finally repeal and replace Obamacare?
- What four actions will conservatives take to move forward?
- Will America go with a comprehensive pro-growth economic plan?
- Will America continue to slash regulations to spur economic growth?
- Will America rein in skyrocketing government deficits and limit national debt?
- Will we protect our national security with tougher immigration laws and better enforcement?
- Will we protect our borders by building a secure fence?
- Will we continue to allow sanctuary cities to ignore the Rule of Law?

After discussing some of the most controversial political issues we face, the book focuses on the upcoming Congressional elections.

What will happen in the upcoming Congressional elections and beyond? In Part IV, this book addresses the upcoming Congressional elections for both the House and Senate and even looks ahead to the presidential election. On the minds of many readers are questions like these:

- Will there be a Blue Wave, Red Wave, or Conservative Wave?
- Will the Republican Party continue to control the House?
- Will the Republican Party continue to control the Senate?
- Will the new Senate be filibuster-proof?
- Will the new Congress be more conservative?
- Will the millennials derail the new Conservative Era?
- Will the new Congress continue with the same leadership team?
- Will the new Congress support the Trump agenda?
- What is the early forecast for the next presidential election?

Also, Part IV explains how and why the good guys win in the end and answers these questions and more:

- How will the good guys win in the end?
- Why are voting integrity and Voter ID necessary for the good guys to win?
- Why will the good guys win in the end?
- Why will American Exceptionalism win in the end?

Sprinkled in between all these questions and answers are eight bold and powerful predictions for America. In addition to these major predictions, I also forecast the following four major, significant, religious and cultural trends of the coming new Conservative Enlightenment:

- The Return to Faith in God
- The Renaissance of Reason
- The Restoration of Education
- The Rebirth of Morality, Freedom, Peace, and Prosperity

America's future is bright, optimistic, and positive! Remember that the good guys win in the end!

Part I

Why were the 2016 Presidential Election Polls "Wrong" about Clinton? Why were the Lameiro Presidential Election Models Right about Trump?

Chapter 1

How Do Polls Work?

Polls seem to pop up everywhere during a presidential election campaign, they even show up frequently in news reports when there are no presidential elections taking place at all. As an example, in years without presidential elections, almost weekly we learn the results of the latest presidential approval polls.

Polls are such an integral part of the news and the media that it's tough to avoid them. You might even ask if the media are obsessed with polls, hanging onto every report of a presidential candidate going up or down two percentage points. Of course, polls are done not just for presidential elections, but for other elections as well. In fact, polls are used to take the pulse of Americans on issue after issue and on ballot question after ballot question.

Let's face it. Polls are an essential part of the 21st century political experience of Americans who follow the news, whether that news is fake news (stories that turn out to be false after more information is learned about them) or actual real news (stories based in truth and on verifiable facts).

So, it makes sense to get a solid understanding of polls, the polling process, and the closely related topics of models, model building, short term trends, long term predictions, and forecasts.

It also makes sense to gain enough of an understanding of these subjects to make informed decisions about how polls fit into the fake news and real news we encounter every day. For example, are the results of a poll reported by the media likely to be highly accurate or just rough estimates? Is it possible the poll is an attempt to make news or influence political opinion rather than report on the mood of voters? What level of credibility can we, and should we, and do we assign to a particular tracking poll?

Indeed, it's good to have an overall knowledge and understanding of the **zeitgeist**, that is, the "spirit of the times" as the German word Zeitgeist translates into English. Americans seek to form general opinions about the times as well to make judgments about the individual news stories we read or hear about every day. To accomplish that, it's vital that we understand polls and the polling process, at least to some degree.

After all, polls are genuinely an integral part of the news. Polls are even frequently "the lead news story." Obviously, we need a filter to assess that news. We need to put polls in their proper context. We need to master the polls, rather than be a slave to polling data and the news stories that are reported along with them.

How many Trump supporters during the 2016 presidential election, for example, felt depressed or down in the dumps when poll after poll portrayed Clinton the likely winner of the election? Were some Trump supporters so convinced that he would lose the election that they stayed home and didn't bother to even vote?

All interested Americans need to understand polls. They are typically a helpful tool. However, they have limitations, and importantly, they can be and sometimes are misleading. Of course, sometimes they are flat out wrong. Or, if not technically wrong, we get the wrong idea from the reported poll results. We will say more on this point later.

Now, let's look at polls and the polling process. No in-depth technical, mathematical, or statistical knowledge is needed throughout this book. But, just some plain old common sense is helpful. Simply, this is a discussion of important ideas that underlie these tools to understand voters and voters' opinions. With an understanding of the pro's and the cons of current polls and the polling process, we are better able to gauge the present mood of the country and its upcoming future.

What are Polls and Tracking Polls?

The idea of a poll is remarkably simple, yet the implementation of a poll can actually be extraordinarily complex for the practitioners of the polling process. In fact, polls can be accomplished with a vast array of different techniques and technologies. They are fraught with perplexing challenges and puzzling problems, and they can be beset with potential errors at every stage of their development. But, most people can readily understand polling results. The results are usually easy to comprehend, although as we said before, those results can sometimes be misleading.

At the 50,000 foot level, a **poll** is simply asking and recording the opinions of a group of people that represent a larger target population. For example, during an American presidential election campaign, many citizens are curious about who is ahead in the race for the White House. It makes sense to conduct polls to find out who is ahead. There's a market for such information. Citizens are just plain curious about who will be their next president.

Indeed, polls are the only practical way to take the pulse of voters. There's no efficient way to contact every likely voter across America and ask who they are supporting for president. Just imagine trying to call about 135,000,000 potential American voters. In fact, such an enumeration of likely voters would be similar to conducting a national census of all Americas. That staggering task is done every ten years by the United States Census Bureau[8] as mandated in Article 1 Section 2 of the Constitution.

A **tracking poll** is a special type of poll often used in presidential election polling that surveys the same group of respondents over a period of time, in part to test if the group's opinions are changing or staying about the same. Tracking polls typically break the entire panel of respondents into subgroups that are surveyed in blocks. All participants are not queried each time the tracking poll is updated. This cuts down on the cost of conducting the poll.

By the way, the term **poll** by itself typically refers to a one time only survey, but sometimes tracking polls are also referred to as polls for simplicity and convenience.

Often, a polling organization, possibly with the support of one of more media firms, sets up a series of questions about the presidential candidates, related issues, or the election campaign itself. Added to those political questions are generally other demographic questions that take the pulse of the respondents, the so-called survey participants.

Demographic questions gather information on these survey participants themselves. Are they male or female? What is their age range? To illustrate, one approach to divide participants by age might be to consider whether a respondent fits into a given generational group by the year they were born. Are they millennials (about 1982 – 2004), or are they from generation X (about 1965 – 1984), or are they from the baby boomer generation (about 1946 – 1964)?[9]

Other obvious demographic questions include their political party affiliation, if any, and their level of education. It is necessary to get answers to these types of demographic questions to assure the poll is getting some type of representative cross-section of the entire electorate. No major segment of voters should be left out. Otherwise, the polling results can be significantly off. A more detailed list of potential demographic categories is incorporated in the IBD/TIPP tracking poll section later in this chapter.

In any poll, the actual questioning and recording of responses from those surveyed will be accomplished typically with the assistance of a surveying organization that does the field work of seeking, collecting, and tabulating the results.

Let's turn our attention next to a few examples of tracking polls actually reported in the media during the 2016 presidential election.

Example 1 – ABC News/The Washington Post Presidential Tracking Poll

During the 2016 presidential election, ABC News and The Washington Post sponsored a tracking poll.[10] Langer Research Associates produced this particular poll with the help of another organization, Abt-SRBI, that in turn was responsible for doing the voter surveying and data collection.

In this example, the latest ABC/Post poll results were reported on November 7, 2016 one day before Election Day. The ABC/Post tracking poll[11] results at that time were:

- Hillary Clinton – 47%
- Donald Trump – 43%
- Gary Johnson – 4%
- Jill Stein – 1%

Remember these results were reported one day before Hillary Clinton lost the election.

This tracking poll was based on 2,220 likely voters surveyed between November 3rd and November 6th. The margin of error was plus or minus 2.5%, which means that the actual election results (if the election were held during this time period instead of the poll) should be expected to be 2.5% higher, 2.5% lower, or somewhere in between, usually with a high degree of confidence.

Many polls set the accuracy of their polls to a 95% confidence level. Simply put that means the actual election results (if the election were held during the given time period instead of the poll) should fall within the stated margin of error of the polling results, 95% of the time.

To make this point even more concrete, consider the above example of the ABC/Post tracking poll in a little more detail. The polling result for Donald Trump was 43%. The margin of error was 2.5%. That means the actual election result for Donald Trump should the election be held in place of the ABC/Post poll would fall in the range of 40.5% and 45.5%. That's 43% plus or minus 2.5%. The probability of this happening is 95% based on the design of the poll.

In general, polling results will have a margin of error calculated by the polling organization. That helps people gauge the poll accuracy. Obviously, the lower the margin of error that a poll has, the more accurate we expect it to be on average. A poll that has a margin of error of plus or minus 2.5% is probably on average better than a poll whose margin of error is plus or minus 5%. Similarly, the higher the confidence level in the polling results, the more accurate we expect the poll to be. A 95% confidence level is preferable to a 90% confidence measure.

Let's pin down these terms further. The **margin of error** tells us how far off the poll might be from the actual answer, if we could poll everyone in the population and all 100% of the population gave us their honest opinion. Note that some respondents might choose not to give out their true political opinions or personal demographic information to a stranger calling on the phone.

Usually, associated with the margin of error is a confidence measure. The confidence measure, or **confidence interval,** as statisticians like to call it, tells us the probability that the actual results of an election should be expected to fall within the range of the polling results, plus or minus the margin of error.

With the ABC/Post tracking poll,[12] the actual poll was conducted using both landline and cell phones and in both English and Spanish languages. Participants were selected randomly.

Example 2 – Investor's Business Daily/TechnoMetrica Market Intelligence (TIPP) Tracking Poll

In another example of a tracking poll, Investor's Business Daily teamed up with TechnoMetrica Market Intelligence (TIPP). The IBD/TIPP tracking poll[13] that surveyed 1,107 likely voters from November 4th through November 7th reported results of:

- Donald Trump – 45%
- Hillary Clinton – 43%
- Gary Johnson – 8%
- Jill Stein – 2%

Their poll had a 3.1% margin of error. In other words, they had a high confidence that the actual election results should the election be held in place of the IBD/TIPP poll were within the range of the polling results obtained, plus or minus 3.1%.

Translated to the tracking poll results, the actual election result for Donald Trump should the election be held during the given time period in place of the IBD/TIPP poll would be expected to fall in the range:

- Donald Trump 45% – 3.1% = 41.9%
- Donald Trump 45% + 3.1% = 48.1%

a 6.2% interval spread with a high degree of confidence.

A typical poll such as the IBD/TIPP[14] poll might include demographic questions that ask the respondent about topics such as those below, and then tabulate the results into pre-selected categories. The list below of demographic questions and categories for answers is largely adapted from the IBD/TIPP tracking poll cited:

- Political Party Identification (Republican, Democrat, Independent/Other)
- Age (18-44, 45-64, 65+)
- Gender (Male, Female)
- Marital Status (Single, Married)
- Education (High School, Some College, College Degree)
- Geographical Region (Northeast, Midwest, South, West)
- Income (Under 30K, 30K – 50K, 50K – 75K, Over 75K)
- Ideology (Conservative, Moderate, Liberal)
- Race (White, Black, Other)
- Ethnicity (Hispanic or Latino, Not Hispanic or Latino)
- Religion (Protestant, Catholic, Other, None)
- Area Type (Urban, Suburban, Rural)
- Union Household (Yes, No)

When you think about it, the IBD/TIPP tracking poll results do not differ markedly from the ABC/Post tracking poll. Donald Trump results were 40.5% to 45.5% in the case of the ABC/Post tracking poll and 41.9% to 48.1% in the IBD/TIPP poll. Yet, the tracking polls differed in the "winner" of the election.

Suppose two different potential voters read the news right before the presidential election. The voter reading the ABC/Post poll might think that Hillary Clinton had the election in the bag with a 4% lead immediately before the election. While an IBD/TIPP poll reader might assume Donald Trump would win the election by 2% of all voters.

Incidentally, Donald Trump's actual election returns gave him 46.1% of the vote tally.[15] The 46.1% number fell within the IBD/TIPP tracking poll range, but it did not fall within the ABC/Post range above. In one sense, both tracking polls were reasonably close to one another in capturing the mood of the country relative to the support voters gave to Donald Trump, since Donald Trump did get about 46% of the popular vote. But, again, both tracking polls implied a markedly different election outcome.

Example 3 – USC Dornsife/L.A. Times Presidential Election "Daybreak" Tracking Poll

Let's next take a look at another tracking poll that often seemed to be out-of-step with the results of many other polls during the 2016 presidential election campaign. The University of Southern California's Dornsife Center for Economic and Social Research and the Los Angeles Times joined forces to develop the USC/LA Times or Daybreak tracking poll.[16]

This tracking poll was updated daily by surveying a subset of the approximately 3,000 U. S. households originally selected as the sample for the poll. To assure in part a representative sample, all the households were selected randomly. After the daily update, results were averaged in with the previous week's responses. You can think of it as a rolling average and update.

The Daybreak poll[17] asked respondents three questions to gauge the mood of the country on the presidential election that were roughly worded as follows:

- What's the percent chance you will vote for president?
- What's the percent chance you will vote for Clinton, Trump,

or someone else?
- What's the percent chance Clinton, Trump, or someone else will win the presidential election?

Incidentally, to avoid introducing a bias into questions #2 and #3, the order of the candidate names are randomized in the surveys presented to respondents. The actual poll was conducted over the Internet. If a selected household did not have Internet access, it would be provided to the household.[18] Again, this was an attempt to include all households and make it a more representative sample of the electorate.

The final Daybreak polling results[19] prior to the election were:

- Donald Trump – 46.8%
- Hillary Clinton – 43.6%

Notice that the Daybreak poll not only correctly picked the winner of the election, but also the winning percentage, namely about 46%. In fact, during the presidential election campaign in the Daybreak poll, Trump consistently ran approximately 6% ahead of his results in other polls.[20]

What was the difference between the Daybreak poll that seemed to favor Trump versus the other polls that appeared to favor Clinton? It's helpful now to learn why the Daybreak pollsters believed they picked the right election winner.

The answer to the Daybreak pollsters was the complex weighting system they used to weight the actual responses. In other words, they didn't treat all polling answers equally. While their weighting methodology was criticized by some during the presidential campaign, it nevertheless provided a high degree of alignment with the actual election results. Plus, it picked the ultimate winner of the election.[21]

Of interest, when the Daybreak polling raw data was weighted more closely in line with how other polls weighted their raw data, the calculated results were fairly close to the results seen by the other polls. As this example illustrates, weighting can be a significant factor in the design of a poll. It helped the Daybreak poll yield the correct winner in the self-assessment of their tracking poll.[22]

What does weighting specifically mean in a poll? **Weighting** is a method to make polling results more representative of the opinions of the population being surveyed.[23] It takes the raw polling data (that is, real data collected from respondents) and weights it by demographic or other factors to make the actual sample seem to match the population being sampled by the poll. The idea is the polling results will then match the electorate more closely.

To show how weighting works, let's take a simple example. According to an article in Politico, there were about 200,000,000 registered voters in America in 2016.[24] Of course, the number of likely voters is a much lower number than that number. If a poll samples 1,500 registered voters and does not take into account whether or not the registered voters will turn out to vote, the results will be skewed. Polls of likely voters in general provide more accurate polling results than do polls of registered voters. One solution to this problem is weighting.

Weighting might be used in this example to account for the over counting of some groups, if the pollster believes they know which groups of survey respondents are less likely to follow through and vote. In this situation, weighting is used to weight or adjust from registered voters to likely voters. After all, if we want to know who will be the next president of the United States, we only care about likely voters, not all those registered voters who sit home and don't vote.

Weighting is related to what I call the underlying model used to interpret polling results. Weighting or more generally modeling is vital to forecasting the electorate. We will discuss these essential topics in more detail later in this book.

With this introduction to polls, it's helpful to understand the process of polling. What steps must a polling organization take to conduct a quality pool?

The Polling Process

Assuming you want to conduct a presidential election campaign poll (or actually for that matter any other poll), you generally need to follow certain steps. In this section, we take a fast look at those steps without the tedious detail that real pollsters face in their day-to-day work.[25]

Let's assume a media organization wants to conduct a presidential election poll among the two leading presidential candidates from the major parties and two other candidates from two other smaller political parties such as the Libertarian Party and the Green Party.

Resource Partners, Plan, and Budget. The first step for the media polling team is to determine the resources it needs to conduct the poll. These include potential additional media partners, polling firms that design the poll, and survey firms that are responsible for asking the political and demographic questions, collecting the responses, and tabulating the results.

In addition to identifying possible resource partners, a detailed plan, the corresponding budget, and approval from management are all needed to get started. It's also necessary to realize these items are not fixed in cement. Other steps that appear below might influence the plan and budget and might also require additional management involvement and approval.

Geographical Scope. The second step is to confirm the final geographical scope of the poll. Does the media polling team want to know who's ahead in the race for the White House on a national level? If yes, the sample population they are polling is the entire electorate. Of course, the ultimate sample size will be much smaller than all registered voters or all likely voters.

Alternatively, the geographical scope for the poll might be just one state. Possibly, the media polling group is a TV station in Cleveland, Ohio and they want to gauge voter support for the leading presidential candidates in the State of Ohio. After all, Ohio is often a pivotal state in presidential election contests and many of their listeners will find such a poll of great interest.

Of course, the media organization might also be seeking information on the presidential race for a single city, like Cleveland, or for a larger area, such as the entire Midwest.

It's up to the media polling team to carefully define the geographical scope of the poll and plan the poll around that key decision.

Frequency and Timing. Next, the media team will likely want to define the frequency and timing of the particular poll. Is it a straight-forward, simple poll or a more sophisticated tracking poll? Will it be done just one time only? Or, will it be done once a week, or once a month, for the duration of the presidential campaign?

Sample Size and General Sampling Approach. In addition, other questions need to be addressed as well. What is the necessary sample size of the poll in question? For example, should the sample reach out to survey 800, 1200, 1500, or even more participants? Also, how will respondents be selected? Some obvious choices include contacting potential respondents by landline phones, by cell phones, or even over the Internet.

Sample sizes are not determined arbitrarily as you might guess. Indeed, pollsters employ some fairly standard statistical methods and formulas to determine the optimum sample sizes. For curious readers, there are many sources to learn more about sampling.[26]

Margin of Error and Confidence Interval. At this step in the polling process, the media polling team needs to have a pollster or statistician calculate the margin of error for the poll and the poll's confidence interval. These will serve to help citizens understand the level of accuracy in the polling results reported.

As we know, the margin of error and the confidence interval are a not a guarantee of precision of polling results. Errors can and do creep in during the polling process.

Representative Sample. Another essential issue for the media polling team to tackle is the representation of the population being polled. To get good polling results, you need to study the opinions of the entire electorate being polled. To illustrate, if you only poll white, college-educated, single women, don't expect the results to be representative of white, high school educated, married men or any other demographic groups for that matter.

Truly, the American electorate is a diverse electorate along many different demographic lines and divisions. Political opinions as we know vary widely. The concept of a representative sample is the attempt by pollsters to achieve a more precise cross-section of our electorate. Thereby, they hope to design polls that yield more accurate results.

At this stage of the polling process, the question is simple. What will be done to assure the survey respondents will be a representative cross-section of all the voters in the geographical area that the poll covers?

Fortunately, as you might imagine, there has been lots of thought and research put into sampling techniques to maximize a fair representation of the target population and to minimize any unfair biases in the procedures.[27]

Weighting Techniques. Another important step in the polling process that follows directly from the attempts to create a representative sample is weighting, a technique we reviewed quickly in our third example above. It turns out that weighting the results of raw polling data to better conform to the electorate is a fairly standard practice among pollsters. Sometimes, the weights used at this stage are collectively called the **weighting model.**

At this stage in the polling process, the polling team needs to consider any factor that might cause the results to be non-representative of the population being surveyed. They also must determine actual weighting that will be used during the process of adjusting raw data to final reported (to the public) results.

After making all these tough decisions in the polling process about the scope, nature, and details of a presidential poll, the tough reality is there are still many practical challenges and issues to overcome before achieving accurate results. Let's highlight some of these issues next.

Polling Challenges and Issues

Here are a list of just some of the questions, challenges, and issues that face pollsters:

- What demographic variables should be included in a poll?
- How should the demographic variables chosen above be weighted in a poll?
- How should poll respondents be categorized as Registered Voters (RVs) vs. Likely Voters (LVs)?
- How should small subgroup samples be determined?
- How should non-responsiveness be handled in the polling process?
- How should biases be eliminated anywhere in the polling process?

Demographic variables might introduce errors into the final results of a poll if the raw data has too many respondents in one area. For example, a common complaint about surveys are the polls that oversample Democrats, or that oversample Independents, and under sample Republican voters in a given poll, thereby reporting results that appear to favor a Democratic Party candidate. Another example might be the case where a given poll oversamples seniors who are likely voters, and doesn't adequately sample enough millennial likely voters. This, too, introduces an inherent bias into the results of the poll.

Obviously, polls that rely on registered voters are not as precise as those that feature likely voters as the group of respondents sampled. Why? Because many registered voters never actually vote due to their busy schedules and personal commitments or to their dissatisfaction and unhappiness over the choice of candidates in a given election. After all, we know many registered voters stay home on Election Day.

To illustrate that latter point, it appears that many registered voters failed to vote for Clinton during the 2016 presidential election campaign simply because they lacked enthusiasm for her candidacy. Trump supporters in sharp contrast, and as Trump rallies confirmed, were widely enthusiastic for the Trump campaign.

While **registered voters** have properly complied with voting laws and are permitted to vote in an election, **likely voters** are registered voters, who have a definite record of voting in previous elections or are thought by pollsters to have a higher probability of voting in the upcoming election.

The next weighting issue listed above deals with small subgroup samples. It might need some further explanation. What is a small subgroup sample and why does it make a difference to a poll's results?

A **small subgroup sample** is any demographic group that is relatively small in the population and only a few individual respondents represent that sample in the poll itself. It's a special case of the representative sample problem that can really throw off the final results of a poll.

Consider an example. Suppose a national presidential poll sample (the actual raw data) includes only one Hispanic millennial woman. If that one presidential preference polling vote is weighted to represent all Hispanic millennial women across America, is it accurately portraying the opinions of all members of that small subgroup? Or, in general, can any small subgroup sample of one or two or even some other small sample of respondents precisely characterize that particular subgroup of voters in the electorate?

In the case of the small subgroup sample above with only one member in the sample, their answer might unduly impact the polling results. Suppose that a small subgroup sample of one respondent switched from Clinton to Trump, does that mean the entire subgroup they represented in the weighting switched too? Using small subgroup samples is rife with problems for the pollster.

Another issue, non-responsiveness, can be a difficult challenge as well. For example, in the 2016 presidential election, some experts and pundits believed that many conservative voters would not respond to media-sponsored polls. Often angry over fake news stories and perceived rampant bias in their political "reporting," those surveyed sometimes chose not to respond to a poll. In these instances, non-responsiveness translates into results that favor the opinions of those who do respond.

Subtle biases can creep into the polling process at any stage of the process. Pollsters need to be self-aware of their own biases and bias within the community of both polling organizations and their media sponsors. Obviously, too, bias can occur in any number of other parts of the polling process from sample selection and weighting decisions, to question wording and even question rotation.

Let's turn now from looking at polling challenges and issues in general, to understanding some classic polling failures, and to understanding the 2016 presidential election polls in particular. Those are the topics of the next chapter.

Chapter 2

Why Were the 2016 Presidential Election Polls So Wrong and Misleading?

Clearly, most people would agree that the crop of 2016 presidential election polls were wrong at worst or were misleading at best. Nearly, every poll indicated Clinton would prevail over Trump. In the month leading up to the election, one poll even reported that Clinton was leading by a staggering 12% nationally. On October 17, 2016, Monmouth University released these definitive results:

- Clinton – 50%
- Trump – 38%

This poll was done considering a four-way race that included the Libertarian candidate Gary Johnson and the Green Party candidate Jill Stein.[28]

Even well-known political forecaster, Nate Silver and the FiveThirtyEight.com website, with the polls-only forecast model on Election Day gave a 71.4% chance of a Clinton win to a 28.6% chance of a Trump victory.[29]

It's easy to understand with such remarkable and lop-sided polling results, why most Americans believed in late October and early November 2016 that Clinton would become the next president. No wonder the pols and pundits, the media and the pollsters, the candidates and campaigns, and importantly, the American people were utterly astonished when Trump became president-elect.

Over recent years in fact, Americans have come to believe that so-called "scientific" polls are a true picture of the electorate. The historic and critical 2016 presidential election was a wake-up call to America. Not only can polls be misleading, but they can be completely wrong in their designation of a likely election winner.

Fake Polls and Fake News?

Many people today believe some news stories are fake news stories, attempting to sway public opinion. In a similar way, some people today believe that some polls are fake polls, intentionally designed to make fake news. The credibility of some media organizations and some polling results has been in question before, during, and after the 2016 presidential election.

Unfortunately, there is nothing to prevent unscrupulous individuals from constructing polls intended to create fake news and to influence voters to stay at home during an election. Alternatively, such polls might be created to increase support for a certain candidate. Citizens can only rely on the reputations of the media sponsors and the actual polling organizations, the integrity of the professionals involved, and the track records of the particular polls in question.

It is worth mentioning that while I believe most pollsters are indeed professionals seeking to do their jobs with the utmost integrity, it is possible that some polls can be manipulated to yield results that the poll sponsors or the poll designers seek to obtain.

But, even though some polls might be fake polls, sometimes polls are simply misleading or downright wrong. Let's look at two famous misleading polls that historically and incorrectly predicted two presidential elections. Both will give us insights into why polls go askew.

One Misleading Poll – Literary Digest in 1936 (Landon over FDR)

From about 1920 to 1936, the Literary Digest conducted presidential polls to see who was ahead in the presidential campaigns of those years. These polls were called **straw polls** and required substantial efforts to create the results. In 1936, as in the preceding years, the Literary Digest sent out postcard ballots to millions of American using phone directories and other lists of potential voters gathered from a variety of sources. In total, they sent out approximately ten million postcards and received about two millions responses.[30] That's quite a large sample size.

Although this approach worked well from 1920 through 1932, the Literary Digest reported in 1936 the following poll results:

- Alf Landon (Republican candidate) – 57%
- Franklin Delano Roosevelt (incumbent president and Democrat candidate) – 43%

How did that compare to the actual election returns? Instead of losing by about 14%, FDR won dramatically by around 24%. The actual elections results were:

- Alf Landon – 37%
- Franklin Delano Roosevelt – 61%

Parenthetically, FDR received 523 electoral votes to Alf Landon's meager eight electoral votes, a true Electoral College landslide.[31]

What caused a successful Literary Digest straw poll system to err so badly after four previous successful polls? Importantly, what can we learn from this classic polling failure?

One thing that can't be faulted was sample size. A sample size of ten million versus today's typical 800 to 3,000 sample size was certainly statistically adequate. But, the large sample size didn't account for the changing nature of the electorate.[32] This was the time of the Great Depression and also the beginning portion of the Constitutional Activism Era (the fifth American Constitutional Era) in our history.[33]

While the sample size was large, the sample was drawn from sources that favored Republican respondents. Phone directories and car ownership lists, for example, tended to represent more affluent voters. FDR drew support from working class voters and the poor. These same groups tended to ignore the opportunity to send back their postcard ballots to the Literary Digest.[34]

We can attribute the Literary Digest polling anomaly to several factors, but two factors seem to stand out. First, the large sample size was not truly representative of the electorate and second, the underlying model of the straw poll didn't account for the changing nature of voters in a new American Constitutional Era.

Note to readers thinking ahead about the 2016 presidential election polls results. America entered a new American Constitutional Era in 2016 just as I predicted in *Great News for America*. This is one reason why the 2016 polls were so far off base. The underlying models didn't adequately account for the changing electorate.

Another Misleading Poll – Gallup Poll in 1948 (Dewey over Truman)

The Gallup Poll in 1948 is another example of an infamous poll with a historically incorrect prediction. The well know photo of a smiling President Truman holding up the newspaper headline: "DEWEY DEFEATS TRUMAN" is memorable among presidential history buffs.[35]

That year, the Gallup Poll predicted Dewey would become president defeating President Truman, who took over the reins of government after the death of President Franklin D. Roosevelt back in 1945. This was the campaign that Republicans promoted the theme: "Had Enough?" They campaigned on eliminating the four C's – Controls, Confusion, Corruption, and Communism.[36]

Gallup accurately predicted the presidential election winners in 1936, 1940, and 1944 with Gallup's method of so-called **scientific polling.** It was a marked improvement over the Literary Digest's straw poll approach because it attempted to choose survey respondents by quota. Of course, it wasn't truly "scientific."[36]

In other words, if 36% of the anticipated or likely voters were high school graduates, Gallup would assure the poll contained 36% of respondents, who were high school graduates. Key subgroups in the electorate were all assigned their quotas. This is known as **quota sampling.**[38]

The flaw in quota sampling was that it didn't represent a more thorough scientific sampling approach. Survey interviewers, who asked the questions, didn't randomly select participants. They were more focused on meeting their quota for each demographic subgroup in the electorate, not on getting a representative sample at the same time. Today, most polling experts probably agree **random sampling** yields more accurate results than quota sampling, all else being equal.[39]

Incidentally, the Gallup Poll results were:

- Dewey – 50%
- Truman – 44%
- Other – 6%

The election returns were quite different:

- Dewey – 45%
- Truman – 50%
- Other – 5%

Once again, the incorrect winner was indicated by a misleading poll.[40] In 1948, the Crossley and Roper organizations made comparable predictions for the election in their respective polls. All three used quota sampling to achieve their faulty results.[41]

With those two misleading polls as a backdrop, we know that misleading and wrong polls can and do happen. Of interest is that polling professionals learned from their mistakes and attempted to improve the science and art of polling. The results of the 2016 presidential election polls will likely improve polling in the future as well.

The key takeaway from both these flawed polls was the necessity to base polling results on an accurate representation of the electorate. Precise polling results are more likely to be obtained when the sample of respondents closely matches the actual voters, who will be voting in the election. Of course, that's easier said than done in the heat of a presidential election campaign.

Oversampling Issues – Good, Bad, or It All Depends?

Oversampling can be a sticky issue in the world of political polling. It can lead to better results, worse results, or different results. In the 2016 presidential election, oversampling was a hot issue. Let's look at the controversy, sift through the arguments, and analyze its likely impact on the 2016 presidential election poll results.

Oversampling is Good. First, let's look at what the proponents of oversampling had to say about its benefits. Andrew Mercer from the Pew Research Center writes about a survey done in June 2016 by Pew Research Center that wanted to study the U. S. Hispanic population in more detail than might be done within a typical polling situation. In this case, Pew roughly doubled the number of Hispanics surveyed, allowing for more in-depth and precise polling results.[42] In general, within statistical limits, the greater the sample size, the more accurate will be the results from a poll.

But, importantly, after focusing on the Hispanic respondents to accomplish their learning objectives, Pew Research decided to weight the total Hispanic survey results back to the corresponding Hispanic numbers in the total poll. Their weighting criteria were based on the U. S. Census Bureau estimates.[43]

Andrew Mercer believed this approach was a good use of oversampling.[44] Indeed, polling larger samples of small subgroups can be one valid approach to dealing with the small subgroup sample problem we discussed earlier.

But, not everyone agreed with the efficacy and effectiveness of oversampling during the 2016 presidential election campaign.

Oversampling is Bad. Take the former mayor of New York City, Rudy Giuliani, speaking on the program Fox and Friends in October 2016 about the presidential election. According to The Washington Times report of that Fox interview, he believed pollsters were oversampling Democrat voters by about 10%, thereby showing Clinton to be ahead in the polls.[45]

Giuliani went on to discuss that pollsters were actually using 2012 models, which was a "totally different kind of election." Plus, he also thought pollsters' voter turnout assumptions about the 2016 presidential election might be off base, just as in the case of the Brexit election.[46] As you probably remember, Brexit was Great Britain's referendum on leaving the European Union. Recall that the Brexit polls showed voters would decide to remain in the EU. However, the actual results yielded the opposite outcome. The Brexit polls were another misleading polling outcome.

Clearly, Rudy Giuliani thinks in this interview that oversampling can adversely and inaccurately impact polls. That certainly can be true.

Let's look at another more contemporary opinion on oversampling.

It turns out that some pundits in 2017 are even tougher on pollsters than Rudy Giuliani was back in 2016. Consider one article that uses the term "flawed methodology" in connection with Trump's presidential approval numbers.[47] This article states:

> "Most of the top political polls that got the 2016 presidential race dead wrong are continuing to use a flawed methodology in rating President Trump's approval ratings that favors Democrats, women and younger voters, according to a new analysis.
>
> The report shows that the mainstream polls oversample an average of 29 percent more Democrats than Republicans and the results skew anti-Trump. The result is that it robs Trump of about 8 points in his approval ratings, from 46 percent to 38 percent, it said."[48]

This article clearly implies that oversampling is being used to mislead and misinform and it's being done on purpose.

Oversampling – It All Depends? Whether oversampling is good or bad in a particular polling situation depends on the context of its usage. It also depends on the integrity and the intention of those conducting the poll as well as those sponsoring the poll. Oversampling can be good or bad.

Was oversampling during the 2016 presidential election campaign done on purpose to thwart the outcome of the election? Was it done to discourage Trump supporters, hoping they would skip voting because it was a lost cause? Was it simply another form of fake news? Was it the primary reason the 2016 presidential election polls were misleading or downright wrong?

Many thought the media and the polls during the 2016 campaign were in the tank for Clinton and were using oversampling as a political weapon. Indeed, that might be a true claim.

Of course, without clear and convincing direct evidence to the contrary, it's probably best to assume no nefarious motives should be attributed to pollsters. Did I just hear my conservative readers sigh out loud? But, after all, Americans have long lived by the adage, "Innocent until proven guilty." Let's give them the benefit of the doubt.

It's entirely possible that some pollsters believed 2016 was a re-run of the 2012 presidential election and using a comparable underlying 2012 type model for computing weights for the raw data was in order. In addition, 2016 pollsters might also have come to the conclusion before reporting the polling results that their voter turnout assumptions were correct too.

Of course, as I discuss in this book, I thought then the appropriate underlying models needed in the historic and critical 2016 presidential election polls were dramatically different than in 2012. In fact, the 2016 and 2012 presidential elections were fundamentally distinct and required a more sophisticated analysis. I also strongly believed that my voter turnout models were much more accurate in predicting the final results of the 2016 presidential election results.

Those are two major reasons why the 2016 presidential election models were wrong and misleading in my opinion.

Next, let's look at some other issues at play in the 2016 presidential election polls.

Weighting Issues

Closely related to the sampling plan and the potential use of oversampling in the 2016 presidential election polls is weighting. When adjusting the raw data taken directly from survey respondents and computing the poll results, weights are often involved. You might think of the weights used in those calculations as the model itself, although a model implies much more in reality.

Suppose a 2016 pollster believed that the electorate was roughly the same in 2016 as in 2008 and 2012 and that Black turnout could reasonably be expected to be about the same. This pollster might then use available data to estimate how many Black voters would actually vote in the 2016 election.

The raw data could be further updated to reflect the pollster's 2016 voter turnout assumptions. For purposes of illustration, the pollster might reason that Black voters are similarly interested in the 2016 election and therefore, they will turnout 98% as often as in 2012.

What is striking to think about in this illustration is the fact that the 98% Black voter turnout assumption could vastly over estimate Clinton's polling results in the polls, if instead the real Black turnout in the election is 92% for example.

In other words, if the voter turnout assumption is overstated in the weighting of the raw data, then the reported polling results will be overstated as well. Sometimes, in fact, a weighting error will be amplified or magnified in the final reported polling results.

Even weights that are slightly inaccurate can turn the polling results significantly off from the actual Election Day outcome.

In my opinion, weighting factors used in the 2016 presidential election poll calculations likely helped to cause the results to be misleading in many instances, and in some cases, to be wrong.

Voter Distrust and Non-Response Issues

Another reason why the 2016 presidential election polls were off base was the growing distrust of the media and the polls they sponsor. According to a Rasmussen Reports survey reported publicly in September 2016, 62% of likely voters thought the news media skewed facts to assist some candidates.[49] In fact, in 2017, distrust of the media continued unabated with about 65% of voters across the political spectrum thinking there is a lot of fake news in the mainstream media.[50]

It's now a new fact of life for pollsters that many potential survey respondents are hostile to polls and distrust both the media sponsors and the reported polling results. Years ago, this was not the case.

This hostility and distrust leads to several unexpected consequences. For one thing, some potential respondents will hang up directly on learning that a pollster in calling, or simply refuse to answer and then hang up immediately. Other potential survey respondents are fearful of giving out their political opinions to strangers, knowing in the case of conservative voters, that conservative opinion holders will often be attacked if their views are known.

The second reason above has been termed the "shy Trump" theory when applied to the 2016 presidential election polls. Parenthetically, I might add that the thought of "shy Trump" voters seems like a strange description to apply to Trump supporters given their enthusiasm at Trump rallies.

Nevertheless, the "shy Trump" theory was the idea that some voters were reluctant to tell pollsters they supported Trump because he was disliked so strongly and vehemently by many voters. Data collected during the election campaign indicated that the impact of this polling phenomenon might have lowered Trump's numbers in polls by about 3% for a time, but dropped as Election

Day neared to roughly 1% or 2%.[51]

A third adverse outcome of voter distrust of polls and their media sponsors is subtle sabotage of polls by giving out partially true or even completely false responses to questions. In other words, some survey respondents seem to take pleasure in faking their answers and indirectly helping to make the media appear to have "egg on their face" if their polls turned out wrong.

Rebecca Goldin had an interesting take on the issue of voter distrust and the disconnect between polling results favoring Clinton and the actual election of Trump:

> "In the 2016 Presidential Election, a large population of people who supported Donald Trump felt some distrust toward the media and toward pollsters ... The models predicting the outcome used various methods to predict who would turn out; they simply may not have had the data to predict a strong turnout by people who weren't, generally speaking, talking to pollsters."[52]

Here is the essential point. It's possible that the 2016 presidential election polls didn't accurately reflect Trump's level of support because enough Trump supporters chose to avoid talking with the pollsters. Voter distrust and non-response issues might have led to higher Clinton numbers in the polls.

It's difficult to determine to what extent voter distrust and non-response issues played a role in the 2016 presidential election polling results that were wrong and misleading. They are, however, probably a contributing factor in the polls going askew.

Issues with Potentially Outdated Underlying Models of the Electorate

It's my belief that one of the top reasons the 2016 presidential election polls were wrong or misleading was that some polls used underlying models in their analysis and computations that were simply outdated. Unless a pollster purposely chooses to report raw data, most polls likely base results on an underlying model. It can be a straight-forward model consisting of demographic data or it can contain assumptions about other critical factors related to the electorate.

Earlier, we mentioned how voter turnout assumptions can impact polling results. To take another illustration, we can create in our underlying polling model a subgroup called "turned-off social millennials" that describe millennials who are concerned with several national social issues. Further, this group might also be characterized as turned-off on the system and are expected to largely sit out an election. Turned-off millennials are, of course, a subset of millennials in the underlying polling model.

Let's say our underlying model indicates that out of all eligible millennial voters, 57.8% millennials will actually vote based on our understanding of turned-off millennials. According to the Pew Research Center, 49.4% of millennials actually did vote in 2016.[53] Assuming the underlying model for the poll used the higher percentage millennial participation, the polling results could be considerably off from the electorate.

A myriad of factors can be included in the underlying model a poll relies upon to compute its final results.

I think many underlying models probably used in the 2016 presidential election polls didn't adequately understand and account for the long range trends, short range trends, and the dynamic electoral changes taking place during the historic and critical 2016 presidential election.

Oversampling issues, weighting issues, voter distrust and non-response issues, and importantly, the issues surrounding potentially outdated underlying models of the electorate, all played into the wrong and misleading results reported by some 2016 presidential election polls.

It's my contention that these problems were foreseeable and that's why my predictions for the 2016 presidential election were as accurate as they were. It's the reason why my early and consistent forecast of Trump's election victory was correct as well. It's also why my Electoral College forecast was reasonably close to the Trump – Clinton anticipated 306 – 232 Electoral College victory.[54]

The Polls, the Popular Vote, and the Electoral College Vote

The actual Electoral College vote taken on Monday, December 19th, 2016 was Trump 304 Electoral Votes and Clinton 227 Electoral Votes. The variances from the expected Electoral College votes were due to so-called "faithless" voters who wanted to stray from the candidates that their respective states supported in the popular vote elections.[55]

The Constitution in Article 2 Section 1 provides that the Electors shall vote for president and vice president. It does not require Electors to vote the way the popular vote goes in a given state. That's a tradition that has evolved since the Constitution was written. The Constitution mandates that the respective state legislatures determine how Electors are selected.

In 2016, in the State of Texas, one Republican elector chose to vote for John Kasich (the governor of Ohio) and another Republican elector chose to cast their vote for Ron Paul (a former Texas congressman and Republican presidential candidate).[56]

On the Democratic Party side, a total of eight Democrat electors attempted to cast Electoral Votes for someone other than Clinton. Three of those were rebuffed by state election officials, so Clinton wound up with 227 Electoral Votes total.[57]

As has been the case in a few presidential elections in American History, sometimes the Electoral Vote and the popular vote for president diverge. The 2016 presidential election was such an election.

This digression points out one final point about why the 2016 presidential election polls were wrong and misleading. They were an attempt to measure popular vote. But, presidents are elected by 538 presidential electors from the 50 states and the District of Columbia. Better polling results might be expected if there were 51 separate polls involved in the analysis, rather than just using national polls.

Technically, among the 50 states, 48 states are normally winner-take-all Electoral Votes based on the popular vote in the respective states. Maine and Nebraska allocate Electoral Votes by a combination of winner-take-all and by Congressional districts. In these two states only, two Electoral Votes are allocated to the winner of the state popular vote and one Electoral Vote is allocated to the popular vote winner in each Congressional district. In 2016, Maine had two Congressional districts and Nebraska had three Congressional districts.[58]

Thus, the presidential elections effectively consist of 56 different popular vote elections (50 state winner-take-all elections, the District of Columbia winner-take-all election, as well as five Congressional district elections). In the absence of cost constraints, pollsters might decide to conduct 56 separate polls, allocate expected Electoral Votes, and then add up the results.

To summarize again, oversampling issues, weighting issues, voter distrust and non-response issues, and importantly, the issues surrounding potentially outdated underlying models of the electorate, all played into the wrong and misleading results reported by some 2016 presidential election polls. Of course, the Electoral College vote ultimately determines the winner of a presidential election. It's really 56 elections and technically should be studied with 50 state polls plus polls for the District of Columbia and the five individual Congressional districts that comprise Maine and Nebraska, not one national poll.

Moving ahead, the next two chapters discuss models in general and my long range models, short range models, and dynamic election models for presidential elections and other political insights.

Chapter 3

How Do Models Work?

Polls are useful and can be helpful in understanding voters, when conducted with integrity, rigorous statistical procedures, and with regard to the cultural, political, and economic climate of the nation. Context is vital and polls are simply tools. But, like most tools, if not used properly, they can cause considerable damage or misunderstanding.

We have looked at polls, the polling process, and some of the issues that might have caused the 2016 presidential election polls to be wrong or misleading.

Let's now turn our attention to models and how models can actually enhance and improve the polling process. In fact, models can facilitate better and more accurate polling results. Plus, models can be used to identify key trends, make substantive predictions, and forecast upcoming events.

What are Models?

When I tell people that I like models, I think people unfamiliar with my field have visions of beautiful men and women walking the runways of New York or Paris. I can understand that fact. For me however, my four decades of attraction to models runs much deeper than any good-looking fashion model. For me, it's also more than the beauty of mathematical and statistical equations that can help to describe the real world, the political elections, or the economy. By the way, don't worry — you don't need to understand any arcane mathematics or complicated statistics to read this book.

What I love about models is the simple fact that they are a fantastic learning tool. For example, people can learn so much about the culture, about the political landscape, and about the dynamics of the economy. Models can be used to address any number of challenges, problems, and questions, in any number of circumstances and situations. In my career, I have had the wonderful opportunity to create engineering models, business models, financials models, economic models, forecast models and more.

Indeed, one of my favorite uses of models is to forecast presidential and Congressional elections. Of course, the same principles I use can be applied to gubernatorial elections or mayoral races or various ballot issues. The mathematical and statistical principles related to modeling can apply to many different real-world applications.

Since we have already explored polls in some detail, let's take a look at models and try to understand how they function in the arena of presidential election campaigning, polling, and forecasting.

To begin with, it's helpful to answer the question: What are models? Models can be mathematical, statistical, physical, software, or even conceptual representations of people, places, or things that exist in the real-world.

Indeed, models can represent many diverse things, such as a model of a new spacecraft about to be tested in a wind tunnel for aerodynamic performance, or a model can be a replica of a complex molecule used for pharmaceutical research. These illustrations are called **physical models,** if they are built out of physical materials. On the other hand, if they are graphical depictions built on a computer screen they might be called **software models.**

Math, Stats, and Other Models (without the Math and Stats)

In our context, a **model** is usually a mathematical or statistical representation of something that exists in the real world. It might be as simple as a weighting model that numerically describes the American electorate by one or more major demographic factors. For example, Gallup reported party affiliation in America during

October 2017 as follows:

- 24% - Republicans
- 42% - Independents
- 31% - Democrats[59]

In effect, this constitutes a straight-forward model of America by party affiliation at a given point in time, in this case, October 2017.

But, models can go far beyond characterizing the real-world in a given moment in time. Models can also project from the present moment forward to the future using **forecast models.**

Or, they can look backwards, as I have done in studying every major presidential election in America's 240-year plus history, to design and define the characteristics of what I term historic and critical presidential elections, and the corresponding American Constitutional Era's in American History that are associated with these presidential elections.[60]

In addition to these **long-range models** that consider approximately 24 to 36 year time periods, I also study **short-range models** that span from about 2 to 8 years, and **dynamic election models** that study factors the can and do happen between about 1 and 24 months before an election.

Models can also slice-and-dice so-called Big Data sets from social media and other sources. **Big Data** is a term used to describe the enormous volumes of data associated with social network sites, like Facebook, Twitter, LinkedIn, and other data sources. Public opinion on key presidential issues as well as current voter attitudes on specific candidates can be gleaned from the huge volumes of information found in Big Data. Plus, it's even possible to discern a variety of short range trends from **social media models**.

Forecast Models vs. Predictive Analytics Models

Closely related to forecast models and social media models, but distinctly different is a tool called **predictive analytics** and related techniques from the world of Big Data. While forecast models take current or past data on many voters and project it forward into the future, predictive analytics tries to better understand what current factors are influencing individual voters to yield their likely future behavior.

Forecast Model Example. To illustrate, let's turn the clock back to June 2016 and assume someone is hoping to shed light on the upcoming November 2016 presidential election. At that point in time, a forecast model might study the behavior of Latino voters in the 2012 presidential election, and project it forward to the 2016 election.

In the 2012 Obama – Romney presidential election, the Latino vote made up 10% of the total electorate and split 71% for Obama and 27% for Romney. A 2016 forecast model version of this data might take 71% of the likely voters projected in the 2016 election and assign it to Clinton, while forecasting Trump's likely voter support to be only 27% of the total likely 2016 vote.[61] That's a simple forecast model assuming the data from a previous election. Many pols and pundits might even consider it a reasonable estimate.

Predictive Analytics Model Example. Instead of this forecast model, let's consider a different approach for modeling the 2016 presidential election in early June 2016. We might want to get a handle on what drives Latino thinking in the Trump – Clinton campaign during the summer before the national conventions. This might help plan what speakers to have and what issues to target during the Republican National Convention and the Democrat National Convention.

We might create a predictive analytics model to study questions similar to these questions. What issues are vital to individual Latino voters? What subtle factors will cause these same individuals to solidify their presidential preferences, or to switch their likely votes before Election Day? Do certain influencers have a proportionately greater impact? Aggregating this knowledge, what do we learn from this predictive analytics model on the outcome of the election?

Incidentally, using models doesn't guarantee accurate election predictions. Modeling is still both an art and a science and the accuracy of the expected results depends on the quality of the model as well as the quality of the data used. Let's look at an example of another type of forecast model that picked Clinton over Trump in the 2016 presidential election.

Example – Moody's Analytics' Model

Moody's Analytics' model picked the correct presidential election winner ever since Ronald Reagan in 1980 — at least up until 2016.[62] Moody's Analytics' model is based on looking at various economic and political factors during the presidential election, such as the economy, gas prices, and presidential approval ratings.

I might add their accuracy from 1980 through 2012 doesn't surprise me. That's because this time period coincides with the previous American Constitutional Era and the electorate in 2016 was significantly different than during the 1980 – 2012 time period. In my opinion, their model might have inadvertently been optimized for the previous American Constitutional Era.[63]

In the 2016 presidential election, Moody's Analytics' model predicted Clinton to carry the pivotal states of Florida, Pennsylvania, and Ohio and win the election with 332 Electoral Votes to Trump's 206 Electoral Votes.[64] Obviously, Clinton didn't carry these critical states and didn't win in the Electoral College.

In sharp contrast, my forecast model predicted Florida, Pennsylvania, Ohio and every other state Trump carried would go to Trump and Trump would win in the Electoral College with 339 Electoral Votes. Interestingly, my model yielded virtually the exact opposite Electoral College results of Moody's Analytics' model. My forecast was close to the actual results.

Modeling and the Repertoire of Model Design Tools

So, to summarize, we can add various Big Data models, social media models, and predictive analytics models to our repertoire of model design tools and techniques that include a vast array of traditional mathematical and statistical modeling tools such as forecast models.

But, that's just the beginning. Models seem to offer a nearly limitless range of alternatives for investigating a question, a problem, a challenge, or a system. Models also provide a bountiful opportunity to understand the electorate in general and likely voters in particular. Plus, they can be a source of reasonably accurate election trends, predictions, and forecasts.

You might want to learn more specifically about how my models worked in 2016 and get answers to the following kinds of questions. How can my long-range, short-range, and dynamic election models be used creatively in a presidential election campaign to shed light on the campaign and the likely winner? Importantly, why were my 2016 presidential election models, trends, predictions, and forecasts so accurate? Plus, can these same types of models also be used to forecast the 2018 Congressional elections and political issues and events in 2018 and 2019?

Before tackling these types of questions in the next chapter, I want to address three other subtle points. One point is that polls often are impacted by their underlying models. The second point is that presidential approval polls also are dependent upon their underlying models. The third point differentiates polls from direct forecast models. I hinted at that point earlier, but I want to spend more time on it now to reinforce its importance in interpreting and understanding the 2016 presidential election polls.

Polls and Underlying Models

Let's return to the forecast model example above that dealt with the Latino vote in the 2012 and 2016 presidential elections.

While it's plausible to use this 2012 model of Latino vote as the underlying model for the Trump – Clinton 2016 race, this approach amounts to using an old model in a considerably different election situation. Of course, as the cliché goes, hindsight is 20/20. Yet, I contend from my modeling of the 2016 campaign that we knew ahead of time this simplified model was going to be inappropriate to utilize in 2016.

Sometimes the approach of using an old presidential election model during a new presidential election campaign yields acceptable results. To work, the assumption that the electorate hasn't changed much from the older election to the newer election must be true. As always, the key is to know when and how the electorate is changing, or if it has changed at all. Let's go back to the Latino voter example and complete the discussion.

If someone did follow that particular 2012 model, they would not have achieved great results in the Latino demographic segment of the 2016 election forecast. Consider the actual results.

In the 2016 election, the Latino vote represented 11% of the overall electorate (up 1% from 2012) and split as follows: Clinton 66% and 28% for Trump.[66] So, Trump got 1% more Latino voters on a total Latino vote that grew by 1%. Clinton's 5% loss of support was more striking than Trump's gain of 1% of support among Latino voters.

Now, recognize a significant point. The simplified forecast model example is wrong on its own merits. It predicted Clinton receiving a higher percentage of Latino votes and produced an inaccurate forecast. But, suppose a polling organization also used the forecast model as the underlying model for weighting its 2016 presidential election poll results. This underlying model would throw the poll results off considerably as well.

The bottom line: polls are usually heavily dependent on their underlying models, whether they are based on voter turnout assumptions and demographic models as in the previous chapter's example, or they are based on forecast models as illustrated in this chapter's example.

If the underlying models upon which the polls rely are wrong, the polling results will probably be significantly wrong as well.

Presidential Approval Ratings

Polls and the relevance of their underlying models also show up in our understanding and interpretation of presidential approval ratings. **Presidential approval ratings** are nothing more than polls whose focus is to determine with a single statistical indicator the support a president has among the American people. Indeed, it is a challenge to capture the sentiment of a nation of over 325 million Americans toward its president in one simple statistic.

Let's look at two examples of presidential approval ratings.

First, let's take an example from Gallup. Gallup.com reports these "Trump Job Approval" results for November 27, 2017:

- % Approve – 37%
- % Disapprove – 56%

Results are based on surveys taken by phone with about 1,500 adults across the nation. The margin of error is listed as plus or minus 3%.[67]

Second, Rasmussen Reports gives these ratings in their "Trump Approval Index History" on November 28, 2017:

- Total Approve – 42%
- Total Disapprove – 56%

To obtain these numbers, Rasmussen conducts a daily tracking poll of about 500 voters and reports them on a 3-day rolling basis. The survey is then based on about 1,500 voters with a margin of sampling error equal to plus or minus 2.5% at a 95% level of confidence.[68]

While the disapproval numbers in these examples taken in roughly the same timeframe are the exact same, namely 56%, the approval numbers are quite a bit different. Why?

Of course, random sampling of respondents might account for the difference of 5% between the two approval ratings. In statistical surveys, this is certainly possible.

Or, it might be the case that the respective underlying models are the cause of the difference in approval ratings. Gallup surveys "national adults." It does not survey registered voters or likely voters. In contrast, Rasmussen uses "likely voters," where likely voters refer to respondents, who will likely vote in the next election.

It turns out that we can expect polling results to differ significantly among polls that are taken among:

- All Adults
- Registered Voters
- Likely Voters

What is the impact of this factor on the results? For one thing, likely voters can be expected to be more involved in political issues in general and presidential politics in particular. Their opinions might be better informed and might be more reflective of how future elections will turn out. Presidents and potential future presidential candidates might be wise to listen more closely to their views.

Other factors discussed earlier might come into play as well, including these:

- Oversampling Issues
- Voter Distrust Issues
- Non-Response Issues

In addition, the use of potentially outdated underlying models might influence presidential approval ratings.

The bottom line is that many of the same issues faced by the November 2016 presidential election campaign polls might still be in play with the presidential approval polls. If that is the case, it is possible that Trump's approval ratings are being understated.

Once again, as with other polls, the underlying models used in a presidential approval survey greatly influences the actual presidential approval ratings. The more reflective the underlying models mirror the voters, the more likely the results are accurate.

Let's look next at my third special point about polls and how they differ from forecast models before discussing the modeling process in presidential elections.

Polls vs. Forecast Models – "Now" vs. Election Day

During the 2016 presidential election campaign, I spoke on many Talk Radio shows about how polls were essentially **point-in-time measurements** of voters. Technically, even tracking polls are point-in-time measurements where the point-in-time is typically a few days or a week. For the moment, let's ignore the accuracy of any given poll. That's a different concern.

Consider the 2016 polls as a snapshot of the electorate, a simple point-in-time measurement of voters. In effect, they measure if the presidential election were held at a given point-in-time, would likely voters support Clinton or Trump or Johnson or Stein (probably randomly presented to potential poll respondents)? To illustrate, on October 17, 2016, CBS News reported the following polling results:

- Clinton – 47%
- Trump – 38%
- Johnson – 8%
- Stein – 3%
- Undecided – 2%[69]

Unlike these polling results, how would a forecast be reported?

On Talk Radio shows during the 2016 campaign, I would discuss my forecast for the results on Election Day. Forecast models yield forecasts that are in the future. They are not current estimates of voter sentiment. They are not point-in-time measurements. They represent where the forecast model indicates the electorate will be on Election Day.

While a poll presents a point-in-time snapshot of likely voters, a forecast attempts to accurately project how actual voters will vote on Election Day. Technically, with early voting in some states, Election Day is a time period of several weeks culminating on the usual Election Day of record.

As you will see, this distinction is critical. Why? Because of some of the factors I consider in my models. Voter intensity is one such factor that can make or break polling results. In the next chapter, we will look at an example of voter intensity.

The bottom line is this point. It's important to remember when listening to polling results that those results are a current point-in-time attempt to measure voter sentiment. Many factors might intervene before Election Day to alter those results. In contrast, a forecast attempts to predict Election Day results before the actual Election Day. It is a prediction of the future that includes factors not included in typical polls.

For now, let's summarize the modeling process and its impact on presidential election polls and forecasts.

The Modeling Process in Presidential Elections

The first step in the modeling process is to determine the purpose of the model. In presidential elections:

- Is the purpose to shed light on potential long-range trends and predictions that are about 24 to 36 years in length?
- Is the purpose to understand potential short-range trends and predictions that range from about 2 to 8 years in duration?
- Or, is the purpose to identify dynamic electoral trends and predictions that will likely impact an upcoming presidential election in about 1 to 24 months?

Dynamic electoral models can include both underlying models used to generate polling results or studies of particular factors such as voter intensity, voter momentum, and voter registration dynamics and their effect on Election Day forecast models.

The second step in the modeling process is to determine the geographical and political scope of the model:

- Is it a national model? Note that this type of model includes all states as if it were a single national election.
- Is it a 56-way national model? Note that a **56-way national model** covers the 50 states separately along with the DC model, and the five Congressional Districts in Maine and Nebraska.
- Is it a simple state model, covering one state?
- Is it a simple Congressional District, city, or county model?

The next step, the third step, is to determine the nature of the model:

- Is it an underlying model to be used as the basis for conducting a poll?
- Is it a model whose purpose is to identify trends or to help make predictions?
- Is it a predictive analytics model to help understand individual attitudes, or to project likely behaviors, or to determine influencing variables?
- Is it a forecast model that will result in an Election Day forecast?

The fourth step is to determine the source of the data:

- If the underlying model is developed for a poll, what is the appropriate data to be used?
- If the model is developed for a forecast model, what dynamic election factors and variables are to be included? What timeframe of analysis is appropriate? What long-range trends and short-range trends are appropriate to include?

Of course, testing, refinement, and optimization of the model design is normally a part of model development as well.

As underlying models for polls, models can actually enhance and improve the polling process. A solid underlying model can greatly impact the accuracy of polling results. Plus, long-range, short-range, and dynamic election models can be used to identify key trends, make substantive predictions, and forecast upcoming events.

Let's next consider why my presidential election models, trends, predictions, and forecasts were accurate before, during, and after the historic and critical presidential election of 2016.

Chapter 4

Why Were the Lameiro Presidential Election Models, Trends, Predictions, and Forecasts So Accurate?

During the 2016 presidential election campaign, I was often asked on-air why I thought my forecasts were accurate despite so many polls predicting Clinton's victory. After the election, I frequently was asked a related question: Why were my consistent and steadfast forecasts of a Trump victory correct when so many polls predicted the exact opposite result? I address those questions in this chapter.

In addition to my presidential election prediction of a Trump victory, I closely predicted the actual Electoral College outcome. In my January 2016 book (written in 2015), I also accurately predicted that the 2016 presidential election would be both historic and critical. I foresaw that it would have historic characteristics such as a change in the mainstream media. Indeed, I made ten predictions that have largely come true or are in the process of coming true.

You might want to learn specifically about how my models worked in 2016. You might want to get answers to these types of questions:

- How can my long-range, short-range, and dynamic election models be used creatively in a presidential election campaign to shed light on the campaign and the likely winner?
- Why were my presidential election models, trends, predictions, and forecasts so accurate?
- Can these models be used to forecast the upcoming Congressional elections as well as political issues and events in the future?

Let's address these questions.

Recall that polls are typically based on an underlying model. It is incumbent on pollsters to use the best possible underlying model for their polls. It is also critical to understand the zeitgeist of the nation, and sometimes the world, in developing the underlying model.

As I alluded to in the discussion of the modeling process in the last chapter, it is important to understand the dynamic election factors and variables that are at play in a given presidential election. Consider one such factor, voter intensity.

Voter Intensity

Voter intensity is a factor I consider vital in presidential election forecasting. Voter intensity is the probability that a likely voter, who tells a pollster they will vote for a certain candidate, will actually follow through and vote for that candidate on Election Day. Obviously, low voter intensity is a bad sign for a presidential candidate and high voter intensity indicates a high probability that the likely voter will actually cast a vote for their candidate.

Looking back at the 2016 presidential election campaign, Clinton's voter intensity numbers were very low, indicating weak support for her candidacy and the likelihood of lower voter turnout on her behalf. Trump, however, had enormous voter intensity as witnessed by the enthusiasm exhibited by likely voters attending his rallies.

My correct forecasting of voter intensity is an example of one reason why my 2016 election forecast was so accurate.

Voter Registration Dynamics

In my world of modeling, **voter registration dynamics** consist of three related factors:

- Total active voter registration numbers by party and by state – What are the baseline registration numbers?
- Rate of change of active voter registration numbers by party and by state – Are they increasing, decreasing, or staying the same?
- Is a positive rate of change of active voter registrations accelerating month-over-month by party and by state?

To take an example, let's look at the State of Florida, a critical election back in the 2016 presidential election and other preceding presidential elections. Current active voter registration numbers by party as of October 31, 2017 were:

- Republican Party – 4,548,627
- Democratic Party – 4,814,215
- Minor Parties – 59,682
- No Party Affiliation – 3,435,109
- Total – 12,857,633[70]

In September 2016, the total active voter registration numbers were:

- Republican Party – 4,500,960
- Democratic Party – 4,800,905

That month, there were 130,371 valid voter registrations and 15,576 removed voter registrations.[71] By the way, if you want to learn more, archived monthly voter registration data by year for approximately the last 20 years is available from the Florida Division of Elections' website.[72]

Regardless of which major party holds the voter registration lead, in a close state, the major party with the highest rate of change of new, valid voter registrations is at an advantage. If the rate of change is accelerating, that's another positive factor. An accelerating rate of change means that each month the actual number of new, valid voter registrations is greater for one party than its increase in the previous month.

Correct forecast for Trump's victory in Florida was in part influenced by the voter registration dynamics in Florida.

Lameiro Presidential Election Models

My model design methodology involves breaking all available data into three major categories based on the time horizon associated with the data as well as the purpose of the particular model design, and then creating appropriate models for each category. The three major model categories I use are:

- Long-Range Models that look at presidential election factors with a 24 to 36 year time horizon
- Short-Range Models that look at presidential election factors with a 2 to 8 year time horizon
- Dynamic Election Models that look at presidential election factors with a 1 to 24 month time horizon

My studies indicate that valuable information that helps understand the American voter typically falls into one of these three major categories of data. It also seems that while a given factor or variable might primarily fit into one category for analyzing the electorate, sometimes it is helpful to include it in another category as well. In this way, it often sheds light on one or more related factors even operating over different time horizons. To illustrate this point, let me show an example.

In my models, political party realignments sometimes show up. Political party realignment is the process where political parties change as a result of voters demanding change in their government. These political party realignments involve major reshuffling of one or both parties and their constituencies. Sometimes, new political parties emerge and old parties die. The

Whigs are no longer in existence, for example.

Political party realignments first seemed to become relevant in my long range models. It is a factor that is seen during American Constitutional Eras when the voters become angry, upset, and frustrated. In my book, *Great News for America*,[73] I discuss the political party realignments associated with various historic and critical presidential elections. As an example, I describe the historic and critical presidential election of William McKinley in 1896 in this way:

> "The year 1896 was a tough year for America. To many citizens, it felt like a year of national crisis. In fact, the immediate years preceding the critical election of 1896 were characterized by political and economic distress and uncertainty among voters. For example, Americans experienced the panic of 1893 that saw about 15,000 businesses go bankrupt. Americans also faced high unemployment, along with political and social unrest.[74]
>
> The political and economic problems America faced before the critical election of 1896 led some voters to even wonder if America and its political institutions would survive.[75] That's how serious the problems were in those days.
> …
> Moral outrage among citizens increased significantly because of the perception that our government was not getting the job done. Citizens often felt that the great economic downturn they were experiencing was not being adequately addressed under the Democratic administration of President Grover Cleveland.
> …
> Political constituencies and support for political parties was clearly and dramatically realigned in the election of 1896 fueled by moral outrage over the state of the union and substantial economic challenges. This realignment would result in Republican presidential election victories throughout the Progressive Era, except for the elections of Woodrow Wilson in 1912 and 1916."

If you think about it, the 1896 presidential election sounds remarkably similar to the events leading up to the 2016 presidential election. Both presidential elections, of course, were historic and critical as I discuss the two in my book, *Great News for America*.[76]

The key point to this example is that the knowledge of the 1896 historic and critical presidential election dealing with political party realignment first shows up in my long range models. Later, it has a dramatic application in my short range models as political party realignment surfaced again in the 2016 presidential election and once again as a factor in the current timeframe. Without a doubt, the political parties are in a dramatic state of flux that will ultimately result in likely major political party realignments. I discuss potential near term political party realignments later in this book.

Let's look at my long-range models, short-range models, and dynamic election models in more detail next.

Long-Range Models (about 24 – 36 years in length)

Long-range models show major changes in American culture, the American political scene and politics, as well as in the American economy that generally occur over a long time horizon. In my research, I have found meaningful long-term results to take place approximately every 24 to 36 years.

I have also detected a long-run repetitive pattern in major cultural, political, and economic activities, behaviors, and events. In fact, it's somewhat stunning to think that major cycles do continue to take place over America's 240-year plus history. The old adage attributed loosely to philosopher George Santayana, "Those who do not learn history are doomed to repeat it," certainly seems to apply in my long-range modeling of presidential elections throughout American History.[77]

Four Bedrock Principles. From my research and efforts in long-range modeling, I believe that the American people have largely been united over our 240-year plus history by four common bedrock principles that are woven into our national DNA and permeate the fabric of our nation. They are morality, freedom, peace, and prosperity.

Americans expect morality in their government. Americans expect their government to promote, protect, and defend their freedom. In addition, Americans expect their government will promote, protect, and defend peace — both external peace with other nations and internal civil peace among fellow citizens. Internal civil peace is evidenced by living under the Rule of Law for all citizens, even the so-called elite. Finally, Americans expect their government to empower prosperity through political and economic freedom, and the Rule of Law by enforcing implied and written contracts.

Of significance is that these bedrock principles (of morality, freedom, peace, and prosperity) largely drive not only long-range cultural, political, and economic trends, but also short-range cultural, political, and economic trends. Dynamic election trends play off these long-range and short-range factors much as a laser beam's photons ride along a fiber optic cable.

Today, it's simply remarkable to see history taking place in front of our eyes. Indeed, we are witnessing American History in our political system right now.

I predicted in 2015 the coming historic and critical presidential election of 2016 largely from my long-range models, but also in part from my short range models. The dynamic election models fed my accurate Electoral College forecast. My associated predictions have largely come true as well.

Long-Range Trends. What are some of the trends learned from my long-range models that fed the short-range models and the dynamic election models, trends, predictions, and forecasts? Here are seven long-range trends:

> **Long-Range Trend #1** – Historic and critical presidential elections are fueled by the moral outrage of the American people.

Background – Voters will become angry, upset, and frustrated when the government doesn't adhere to basic morality or when it infringes upon their freedom. Then, voters will get passionate and will express their emotions at the ballot box.

Long-Range Trend #2 – The moral outrage of voters inevitably leads to political party realignments.

Background – Political party realignments can take a variety of forms. Sometimes a combination of different realignment activities can take place.

Examples – Sometimes political party leaders are replaced. Sometimes political party constituencies are dramatically added, subtracted, altered, or changed. Sometimes new parties come into existence and sometimes old parties die out completely. The American voter is ultimately sovereign.

Long-Range Trend #3 – Historic and critical presidential elections occur roughly every 24 to 36 year in American History.

Examples – Among all eight historic and critical presidential elections are Thomas Jefferson in 1800, Abraham Lincoln in 1860, William McKinley in 1896, and Donald Trump in 2016.

Long-Range Trend #4 – Historic and critical presidential elections always bracket American Constitutional Eras.

Example – The Jacksonian Era that began in 1828 with the historic and critical presidential election of Andrew Jackson and ended with the 1860 historic and critical presidential election of Abraham Lincoln

Long-Range Trend #5 – Closely tied to these historic and critical presidential elections are years of Supreme Court

Constitutional decisions that follow a common philosophical jurisprudence. I term these blocks of Supreme Court decisions as American Constitutional Eras.

> Examples – The Constitutional Era from 1800 to 1828, the Constitutional Activism Era from 1932 through 1964, and the new Conservative Era that just started in 2016.

Long-Range Trend #6 – A new mainstream media usually arises before, during, or after an historic and critical presidential election.

> Examples – New mainstream media examples include the newspaper in 1828, the urban press and magazines in 1896, and the new media, social media, and the blossoming of Talk Radio in 2016.

Long-Range Trend #7 – Along with the above trend, the old mainstream media of the time loses significant power and influence, and eventually its business model falters and fades as well.

> Examples – The demise of the political pamphlet in early America and the end of the mainstream media in 2016 and its ability to influence and shape American presidential elections. Closely tied to the decline in the old mainstream media today is their loss of credibility and their eroding business model.

Long-Range Predictions. Looking at these seven long-range trends, it is easy to see how I could make the ten predictions I wrote in my book, *Great News for America*.[78] The book's launch was in January 2016 just in time for the 2016 presidential election primaries and caucuses.

Not surprisingly given my long-range models, I predicted the moral outrage of the American people going into the 2016 presidential election was so strong that it would result in an historic and critical presidential election. In fact, I predicted it would most resemble the historic and critical presidential election of William McKinley in 1896.

I also predicted it would be a surprising, and for some a shocking, presidential election with events not seen in recent presidential elections. All of these predictions were true. My long-range models anticipated these events.

Incidentally, my long-range trend #3 that predicted the next historic and critical presidential election would take place in 24 to 36 years from the Ronald Reagan election in 1980 also came true. The 2016 presidential election was precisely 36 years after Ronald Reagan was elected president.

In *Great News for America*, I also predicted the coming political party realignments. Specifically, I foresaw the end of both the Republican Party as we have known it as well as the Democratic Party as we have known it. That the two parties have changed enormously during the 2016 presidential election campaign is unquestionable. I think the complete political party realignment is still taking place as later chapters in this book will explore.

As a result of the historic and critical presidential election I anticipated in 2016, using long-term trend #4 I realized we could expect a new American Constitutional Era. Given the short-range models indications that voters were supporting more conservative candidates in 2016, I predicted the new American Constitutional Era would be called the Conservative Era.

Closely related to that prediction, I also predicted the more conservative new president would select four new Constitutional conservatives for Supreme Court Justice appointments during his term. President Trump has subsequently followed through in 2017 with one new Supreme Court appointment, Neil Gorsuch, who is a Constitutional conservative.

Plus, there are strong indications that three more justices, Ruth Bader Ginsberg, Anthony Kennedy, and Stephen Breyer, might retire in the near future. This would mean my prediction of four new conservative Supreme Court justice appointments would indeed take place. Also, it would allow my on-air prediction to come true that there will be a Supreme Court with a super-majority of conservatives during this new president's term of office.

Another set of long-range predictions I made was the demise of the then mainstream media and the rise of a new mainstream media, consisting of the new media, social media, and Talk Radio. The evidence that this set of predictions is coming true is pervasive and ubiquitous. We read stories about old mainstream media layoffs and reductions. We also see our president using social media in the form of tweets in a manner no previous president has ever done.

It is clear how my long-range models of America's 240-year plus history of presidential elections led to my long-range trends and predictions that turned out to be largely true. Let's look next at my short-range models and see how those models fared in my 2016 trends and predictions.

Short-Range Models (about 2 – 8 years in length)

As you might expect, **short-range models** reflect shorter range trends in the general culture, in the political climate and more recent elections, and also in the economic mood of the nation. The time span for most short-range models fit from 2 to 8 years in length.

Short-Range Trend #1 – Conservative Election Trend. One example of such a short-range trend is the conservative election trend from 2010 through 2014. Recall the historic House of Representatives election of 2010 in which 63 House seats turned Republican, followed by the Senate Republican rout in 2014 and the Republican Party taking control of the Senate that year. This pattern riding on top of the long-range trend #1 above dealing with the moral outage of American voters signaled a growing conservative sweep of political offices.

The presidential election of 2012 did not follow, and in fact, broke out of the conservative pattern of the House landslide of 2010 because Romney was not deemed by most voters to be a true conservative. If a conservative Republican had been nominated rather than Romney in 2012, Obama would likely have suffered an electoral defeat.

The level of moral outrage going into the 2016 presidential election was so great that any reasonably conservative presidential candidate would have won the election with a comfortable Electoral College margin. A rock-solid ideological conservative might have prevailed in the Electoral College with even a slightly greater Electoral College edge over Clinton, who did not inspire her own base and even alienated some Sanders supporters in the primary. However, Trump more than adequately addressed the electorate's need for a conservative president, who was also a populist.

Short-Range Trend #2 – "Taking the Fight to the Arch-Enemy" Trend. As we indicated earlier, Trump received 305 Electoral Votes and was seen by voters as a "popular conservative," someone who would take the conservative fight to the Democratic Party's presumed presidential candidate, Clinton, and someone who would most importantly take the fight to the arch-enemy of conservatives — the then mainstream media.

Over America's 240-year plus history, voters often selected military leaders to be president. George Washington was General and Commander-in-Chief of the Continental Army when America fought the Revolutionary War. In the early 1800s, Major General Andrew Jackson gained fame fighting in the War of 1812. William Henry Harrison, our ninth president, was a Major General and the hero of the Battle of Tippecanoe.[79]

Other military leaders that went on to become president included: Zachary Taylor, Franklin Pierce, Andrew Johnson, Ulysses S. Grant, Rutherford B. Hayes, James A. Garfield, Chester A. Arthur, Benjamin Harrison, and Dwight D. Eisenhower.[80]

Who would be better to lead the fight against the then mainstream media than a military leader of national prominence?

Short-Range Trend #3 – "Another General Patton" Trend. While not a general or other military leader, Trump's rough and tough style caused him to be viewed much like Teddy Roosevelt of Rough Riders fame, or like General George Patton known for his pragmatic, demanding style and tough words. One quote of General Patton is relevant here: "Moral courage is the most valuable and usually the most absent characteristic in men."[81]

In 2016, American voters sought moral courage in their president, a president who would fight for conservative principles and for morality, freedom, peace, and prosperity. Trump won the Republican nomination to lead the fight and address America's moral outrage with the government and the establishment elite.

Besides his toughness, Trump qualified with voters as sufficiently conservative to allow the short-range #1, conservative election trend, to continue.

What are some of the other trends learned from my short-range models that fed the dynamic election models, trends, predictions, and forecasts? Here are a few other short-range trends:

Short-Range Trend #4 – "Repeal and Replace Obamacare" Trend. This theme began in the spring of 2010 after the Democrats somehow cobbled together enough votes to pass the so-called Affordable Care Act in March 2010. At the time, it passed with no Republican support and most Americans rejecting it by about a 60% majority. For example, a CNN Opinion Research poll at the time found a 59% opposition to Obamacare.[82]

Short-Range Trend #5 – "Protect Us from Terrorism" Trend. This theme and trend varied in intensity and prominence among the short-range trends preceding the 2016 historic and critical presidential election. After several terrorist attacks, this trend dominated many voters' minds. For example, the Paris attack on November 13, 2015, in which 130 people were killed and literally hundreds more were injured,[83] so concerned Americans that the topics of terrorism and protecting America from similar terrorist attacks dominated how Republican presidential candidates were viewed.

Republican presidential candidate Ben Carson, who had a dynamic electoral bump in primary support, largely dropped from the political radar after he was perceived as weak on terrorism.

Short-Range Trend #6 – "The Economy is Hurting Americans" Trend. Another short-range recurrent theme before and during the 2016 presidential election was the economy and how it was hurting most Americans. Citizens were saying: "We need help. We need jobs. We need action, not words." Clearly, after the 2008 recession, the economic recovery (if you can even barely call it that) was lackluster and far from robust.

The American Economy was definitely in the doldrums and consistently registered as one of the top two trends in likely voters' minds.

Short-Range Trend #7 – "Protect America's Borders" Trend. This theme while significant was not at the top of America's concerns. The threats posed by America's unprotected borders and illegal immigration actually encompassed three major related concerns:

- Terrorists, drug lords, and violent criminals coming into the U. S.
- Diseases and epidemics migrating across our borders
- Real economic burdens imposed by illegal immigrants on our healthcare, welfare, education, and criminal justice systems

Besides the obvious national security threats listed above, likely voters were also apprehensive about the actual economic burdens placed on our healthcare, welfare, education, and criminal justice systems by illegal immigrants. One estimate from the Heritage Foundation at the time was that illegal immigrants cost the government $60 Billion annually in net benefits, over and above, any possible taxes illegal immigrants might pay.[84]

With this as a summary of the short-range trends preceding the 2016 presidential election, let's move onto the dynamic election models that fed my accurate presidential election forecasts.

Dynamic Election Models (about 1 – 24 months in length)

Dynamic election models provide partial or complete Election Day forecasts. To illustrate, a partial dynamic election model might forecast how many men and women will likely vote in the top 10 states (by Electoral Votes) that account for 256 Electoral Votes in total. The Electoral College requires a winner to get a minimum of 270 Electoral Votes. Note that it is a partial model because it doesn't include all 50 states plus D.C. and it doesn't even project winners in those top 10 states. It only yields an intermediate and partial result.

In sharp contrast, a dynamic election model that forecasts winners in a 56-way national model predicts the presidential candidate that wins in each of the 50 states, plus D.C., plus in the five Congressional Districts that make up Maine and Nebraska within the Electoral College. That's a complete dynamic election forecast model. Of course, that's precisely the result most people probably really want, even if they don't realize it. Americans want to know who the president is going to be for the next four years.

Dynamic elections models can kick into use about 24 months before an election. Of course, they can be initiated anytime up until about one month preceding the election to be modeled. But, because of the effort involved, it will probably commence months or years before the Election Day being modeled.

The purpose of dynamic election models is to get an accurate read on the voters who will determine the outcome of the election. Specifically, it seeks to get a good handle on who will vote (in total) and how they will vote (by candidate). To get the correct winner, it must forecast the Electoral College winner, not the popular vote winner, since the president is elected by the Electoral College when it gathers following a general election.

Incidentally, the Electoral College meets by state Electoral College delegations in their respective state capitals on the first Monday following the second Wednesday in the December following Election Day.[85] The District of Columbia casts its three Electoral Votes not in any state capital, as you might guess, but within the

District of Columbia itself.

While a poll focuses on a point-in-time measurement of respondents and their presidential candidate preferences during a presidential campaign, a dynamic election model attempts to predict with some degree of precision the actual outcome on Election Day.

You can think of a complete dynamic election model of the Electoral College winner to be designed in stages. It is, as you might expect, a somewhat complex and convoluted process. It can be implemented and designed with as many stages as the model designer choses, and because of its complexity, it can be subject to potential budget constraints.

While math and stats geeks might prefer the complete detail to be shown below, most of my on-air listeners and readers would probably have their eyes glaze-over, if I attempted to explain this model design process in mind-numbing detail. Here is a quick overview of my approach for those who want to stay awake and finish reading this book.

Dynamic Election Model Stage #1 – Baseline Population Model. The complete dynamic election model starts with the design of the baseline population model. For a 56-way national model, the population needs to be broken down by demographics chosen for all 56 actual elections taking place on Election Day.

Dynamic Election Model Stage #2 – Long-Range Trends Overlay Model. At stage #2, we choose which long-range trends to include in the stage #2 model. We can choose all of them, or just some of them for simplicity, or none of them, if no long-range trends appear to apply during this presidential election cycle. Then, the long-range trends are quantified and superimposed on the baseline population model. Note that long-range trends typically alter the baseline population model, which means the model is already predicting a slightly different set of potential voters.

Dynamic Election Model Stage #3 – Long-Range + Short-Range Trends Overlay Model. This is exactly the same process as the previous step except we choose which short-range trends to incorporate into the updated overlay model from stage #2. Once again, the new overlay model reflects a twice-updated baseline population model of potential voters.

Dynamic Election Model Stage #4 – Dynamic Election Factors Impact Model. At this stage, we add in some or all of my chosen dynamic election factors from a number of factors that are available for this purpose. Some of these dynamic election factors have already been discussed in this book. They include:

- Voter Intensity
- Voter Turnout
- Voter Turnoff
- Voter Momentum
- Voter Registration Dynamics
- Voter Enthusiasm
- Voter Optimism
- Voter Peace and National Security Perception
- Voter Prosperity and Economic Security Perception
- Voter Presidential Candidate Personality Perception
- Voter Fraud

Some of these dynamic election factors were derived from my "Ten Laws for Winning Presidential Elections" that I wrote years ago.[86]

Dynamic Election Model Stage #5 – Forecast Model. Finally, at stage #5, the newest overlay model from stage #3 is joined to the dynamic election factors impact model from stage #4. This process results in an Electoral College forecast.

The whole point of this potentially complex and elaborate analysis is to understand the electorate going into the presidential election and at the end of this process to develop an accurate forecast of the presidential election winner.

The Key to Accurate Presidential Election Models

The purpose of any model is to gain understanding and insight into the system being studied. With presidential elections, models can act as the underlying foundation (the so-called underlying model) for a presidential poll or they can form the basis of a forecast for the winner of a presidential election.

In either case, the key to accurate presidential election models is understanding the electorate. In my view, it is not sufficient to just take generic demographic data from past elections and assume the electorate is static. Just as static models, in my view, don't yield as good an economic forecast as do dynamic models when studying economic growth policies for America, static demographic models for presidential election models are similarly less accurate.

Why were my presidential election models, trends, predictions, and forecasts so accurate in 2016? Simply, my models provided more understanding and insight into the electorate.

Using my long-range models and short-range models, accurate trends appeared naturally from the data. When the trends reached a given level of confidence, it then became easy for me to make reasonable predictions with a high degree of certainty as well. Finally, my dynamic election models captured the effects of voter-related, vital factors that influenced the election outcome when we were within a few months of Election Day.

The powerful combination of long-range models, short-range models, and dynamic election models provided an accurate forecast of Trump's election victory in 2016.

Let's turn our attention now to the political party realignment of America's two major political parties that started with the historic and critical presidential election of 2016 and that continues today.

Part II

What Will Happen to American Political Parties in the Coming Years?

Chapter 5

How Will Current Trends Impact the Democratic Party?

With the 2016 historic and critical presidential election, the Democratic Party reached one of its lowest points in about a century. It is out of power nationally. It relinquished control of the House in 2010 in a 63-seat landslide, the Senate in 2014 in a 7-seat election rout, and the White House in 2016 in an election Democrats thought would be a slam-dunk victory. But, that's not even the whole story.

In the summer of 2017, West Virginia's Democrat Governor Jim Justice switched his party affiliation to the Republican Party. That meant, Republicans held 34 governorships, while Democrats held a scant 15 governorships across America.[87] The 50th governorship was held by Bill Walker from Alaska, who is an independent.[88]

In addition to holding nearly 70% of all governorships, on December 1, 2017, Republicans controlled a remarkable 67 state legislative chambers compared to 31 held by Democrats.[89] That's a total of 98 state legislative chambers. You might be saying to yourself that's two short of 100. Don't we have 50 states? Shouldn't there be 100 state legislative chambers (50 State Houses and 50 State Senates)?

If you don't live in Nebraska, you might not have remembered that Nebraska is the only unicameral legislative state in America. Since it was first implemented in 1937, Nebraska has had just one legislative body and it's nonpartisan. Neither the Republican Party nor the Democratic Party control the Nebraska unicameral legislature. Incidentally, political candidates running for legislative office in Nebraska don't even have their party affiliations listed on the ballot.[90]

Another way to view the decline of the Democratic Party across America is to look at those states in which one party controls the governor's mansion plus both state legislative chambers — what has been called a "state government trifecta."[91]

Before the 2010 elections, the Democratic Party controlled 17 such states: Maine, Vermont, Massachusetts, New York, New Jersey, Delaware, Maryland, West Virginia, North Carolina, Arkansas, Wisconsin, Illinois, Iowa, Colorado, New Mexico, Washington, and Oregon.[92]

In 2017, the Democratic Party had only eight state government trifectas: Connecticut, Rhode Island, Delaware, Washington, Oregon, California, and Hawaii.[93] That represents a significant loss of control for a political party at the state level.

Plus, consider the dramatic decline in Democratic Party presidential primary voters from 2008 to 2016. In 2008, about 38 million voters participated in the Democratic Party primaries vs. the deflated 31 million voters who came out to support both Clinton and Sanders and a few others. That shows a downward spiral in Democrat voter participation and support. It also helped foreshadow Clinton's loss in November 2016.[94]

Truly, the Democratic Party faces some stark electoral math. In addition, the Democratic National Committee fundraising has been anemic and the Democratic state party organizations have floundered across America under Obama's centralized political strategy and nationalized organizational regime. Democratic Party leadership, too, generally rests on the shoulders of old politicians and those near retirement.

The keys to political success include leadership and vision, management and strategy, people and organization, as well as communications and money. When multiple pillars of political success are damaged, lacking, or virtually non-existent, election losses are inevitable.

With presidential elections, the calculus of the Electoral College requires special attention. Consider today's political reality for the Democratic Party.

The Electoral College Favors Heartland America over Coastal America

No doubt about it. The Democratic Party faces an Electoral College that favors the Republican Party. Just think. If you take the Left Coast plus Hawaii and add it to roughly the Northeast from Maine to D.C., the Democrats can cobble together about 170 Electoral Votes of the 270 Electoral Votes necessary to elect a president. Michael Barone calls this Coastal America.[95]

In sharp contrast, the Republicans hold an electoral competitive advantage in the Midwest, South, and Southwest states, along with Alaska and Pennsylvania, two states that much prefer Republican energy policies. This group that Michael Barone terms Heartland America for obvious reasons represents a significantly powerful 368 Electoral Votes.[96]

But, of course, Democrats might counter that they can win in states like Colorado, New Mexico, Nevada, Minnesota, and Illinois with a total of 51 more Electoral Votes. But, even if it they can carry these states in the future, their total Electoral Votes fall far short of the needed 270 Electoral Votes necessary to regain the White House.

The reality is that many Democrats prefer to live in big cities and on the coasts, while Republicans prefer suburban and rural areas in fly-over country. Concentrating their electoral strength in a few larger cities is clearly not an Electoral College winning strategy as the Founding Fathers sought to dilute the power of the Federal government by increasing the power of the states.

The Electoral College will continue to move in a more conservative direction and then stay there for 24 – 36 years. This prediction does not favor growth of the Democratic Party, but rather it favors the further decline of the Democratic Party.

Small Political Contributors Favor Republicans over Democrats

The electorate still seeks to take on the establishment in Washington, D.C., and drain the swamp. As a result, small political contributors to the Republican National Committee are taking on the normally larger donors in the Republican Party as a meaningful political factor. In 2017 through August 31st, small political contributors donated more than $40 million to the Republican National Committee vs. small Democratic Party donors that gave only $25 million to the Democrat National Committee. By the way, small contributions consist of gifts of $200 or less.

Of course, these donations are significant because money can and does get the attention of politicians; it can and does influence political positions on issues; and ultimately, it can and does impact policy formulation and legislation.

Small contributions to the more conservative political party and to conservative political candidates will continue to increase in total dollar value and in total number of contributions. Note the use of the term "more conservative political party." It is used intentionally in the event the Republican Party changes as we will discuss in a later chapter.

More Red Pills are being Swallowed than Blue Pills

You may remember from a science fiction movie called The Matrix that red and blue pills play a key role in that plot. The idea of a red pill is that it gives the person who swallows it freedom, truth, and the knowledge of reality. The opposite of the red pill is the blue pill. When taken, it bestows upon the person taking it a false sense of reality and security. The analogy to our political world is striking.

Of course, the red pill represents the traditional American values that follow the Declaration of Independence, the Constitution, the

Rule of Law, morality in government, freedom (religious, political, and economic), limited government, and a strong national defense.

In contrast, swallowing the blue pill means you are opting for the security of a big, controlling government. But, that security comes at a hefty price, the loss of your knowledge of reality, and the loss of your individual freedom. In place of the truth and your knowledge of reality, when you take a blue pill, you must accept socialist narratives and fake news that foster government control.

When a person says they have swallowed the red pill, it means they have rejected progressive and socialist ideology, especially totalitarian and radical tactics, in favor of the four bedrock principles of morality, freedom, peace, and prosperity.

Surprisingly, many progressives are getting turned off by some of the antics of the Left and especially the alt-Left. Attempts by the Left and their allies to shut down free speech on college and university campuses and in other venues is upsetting many traditional liberals. While progressives might be sympathetic to big government causes, they reject totalitarian and radical means to advance progressive socialism. In other words, the loss of free speech to obtain more government control over our lives seems too high a price to pay for many who used to support the Democratic Party.

The number of people figuratively swallowing red pills (that is, becoming conservative) will accelerate and then level out at a comfortable plateau in the next 24 – 36 years. Since support for progressive socialism is closely tied to the Democratic Party today, this does not bode well for the long-range viability of the Democratic Party.

Identity Politics is in Decline
The Democratic Party has largely invested its strategy and political future in identity politics. **Identity politics** is the frame of reference some social groups use to view their world and use to organize their sense of perceived and shared injustice, victimization, or oppression.[97]

Of potential interest, some philosophers believe identity politics has evolved over the past several decades as a direct consequence of the sexual revolution. Why? It has evolved because of the decline of the family as a psychological buffer and support system for the stresses and strains of life. Identity politics fills in the emotional gaps left in people's lives.

Damaging factors such as: "No-fault divorce, out-of-wedlock births, paid surrogacy, absolutism about erotic freedom, disdain for traditional moral codes ..."[98] contribute to the breakdown of the family and its positive social and psychological support systems for many people. This in turn seems to be associated with identity politics. However, while many of these factors continue to persist, there is nevertheless a trend toward restoring the family as the fundamental unit of civilization.

The Democratic Party reaction to the identity politics phenomenon has been to encourage and support it. Consider, for example, both Obama and Clinton's support for the politics of victimization. In addition, the Democratic Party has concurrently abandoned its traditional strategy for engaging and supporting working-class voters, especially white non-college graduates. This is a political blunder of seismic proportions.

How has their strategy played out? The Democratic Party strategy in recent years has largely been centered on expecting the support of unmarried women, millennials, and non-white voters. These groups have been termed the "rising American electorate"[99] and "ascendant America"[100] because pollsters believe these groups will increase in numbers. Democrats thought these voters would be the core of electoral success, including in 2016 for Clinton.

Democrats inaccurately made two assumptions about the so-called ascendant Americans. First, they assume that these potential voters will go to their polls and cast votes. Second, they believe they these potential voters will vote *en mass* as a monolithic bloc. The reality is that these groups aren't necessarily getting out and voting in the numbers anticipated by some political pundits. Plus, when they do go out and vote, they are increasingly splitting their loyalties among different political parties. That turns out to be more bad news for the Democratic Party.

Some progressives argue the Democratic Party needs to drop the strategy of identity politics and switch to a strategy and messaging with more of a working-class economic theme.

The bottom line is that identity politics is in decline, both as a useful electoral strategy for the Democratic Party at large and as a reality within American politics. Members of identity groups of the past are self-identifying less and less with their assumed identity groups. But, it will take time for this to play out.

Tribal Politics is on the Rise

In contrast, **tribes** are groups of people who self-identify more with their shared values and shared lifestyles than they do with their traditional ethnic, religious, cultural, regional, age, or income ties.[101]

For example, a middle-age single man of German and Lutheran ancestry with strong conservative, family ties growing up, who works in software development in Cupertino, California, might not relate to his age cohort, might not relate to his German ancestry, might not relate to his Christian heritage, and might not relate to his conservative and family roots. Instead of feeling a close part of his traditional demographic groups, he might instead belong to a virtual community of shared values with a shared lifestyle.

This virtual community might live within 100 miles of Silicon Valley and be characterized by single adults who date serially and rarely get married, hold atheistic or agnostic views of God, consistently hold onto progressive political views, enjoy wine and cheese parties, participate in hiking and skiing, and join other like-minded individuals in various MeetUp social activities. For those, who are unfamiliar with Meetup.com, according to its website: "Meetup brings people together to create thriving communities."[102]

At first, you might think the dual trends of moving away from identity politics and moving toward tribal politics favor the Democratic Party. But, it's just the opposite. In the past, identity groups had an exceptionally strong loyalty to the Democratic Party. In contrast, tribes are much more likely to splinter and re-cluster among different political parties and varying political candidates. Clustering occurs within tribal groups based on their shared values and lifestyles. Plus, this clustering can evolve over time.

The future impact of tribal politics seems to reinforce and overlap the identity politics trend discussed above.

Tribal politics will increasingly impact political elections in the new Conservative Era. Members of identity groups are increasingly embracing membership in shared value and shared lifestyle tribal communities that in turn, are increasingly conservative in both their values and lifestyles.

The Left's Power Coalition is Imploding

For decades, the powerful left-wing political structure in America was run by a coalition of power brokers from the Democratic Party, the old mainstream media elite, Hollywood liberals, university socialist and Marxist professors, left-leaning union officials, plus some wealthy leftist donors.

The Left's power coalition was a forceful and formidable cartel that dominated American left-wing politics for years. It bullied, cajoled, shamed, and dragged many Americans into politically correct compliance with its vision for:

- Implementing progressive socialism,
- Reducing traditional family values and sexual morality,
- Promoting a radical sexual revolution,
- Enervating the Constitution,
- Reducing equality under the Rule of Law,
- Restricting individual religious, political, and economic freedom,
- Increasing government size, role, and power, and
- Rejecting the long-held belief in American Exceptionalism.

The reality is that the Left's power coalition is imploding. Look around at the damage and the destruction. It's self-evident.

The power and standing of the Democratic Party has been decimated as catalogued earlier in this chapter. Offices held across the country by Democrats have dramatically declined. They have lost the White House as well as the House and the Senate. They have lost most governorships and most state legislative chambers. The losses continue to mount for the Democratic Party.

The old mainstream media has lost a considerable portion of its credibility. When a new negative story on the Trump administration is released by the old mainstream media, the response by many viewers or readers is to ask whether or not this might be another "fake news" story. Their socialist narratives are no longer taken at face value.

Consider just three examples of "major news" stories that turned out to be false in about one week alone. To start with, ABC News reported in a blockbuster story that Michael Flynn was prepared to testify that President Trump, while still a presidential candidate, directed him to contact Russians. That "major news" proved false.

In a second example, Reuters and Bloomberg incorrectly reported that the Special Counsel Mueller's office had subpoenaed President Trump's financial records, another potentially significant story that turned out to be false. In a third example of false news in about a single week, CNN reported that senior Trump campaign officials were tied to unreleased WikiLeaks documents.[103]

These types of stories in the old mainstream media certainly lend support for the idea of fake news and readily explain why the old mainstream media continues to lose its credibility. The old mainstream media's business models are also deteriorating. Layoffs, downsizing, staff cuts, and office space reductions are no longer surprising.

Evidence of the Left's power coalition implosion is not limited to the Democratic Party or the old mainstream media. Consider Hollywood liberals. The Hollywood elite have been known for their consistent support for leftist causes, regular left-leaning testimony when called before Congress, campaign help for left-wing political candidates, and substantial financial backing for all things Left.

What has happened to this powerful group of leftists?

The ranks of the Hollywood liberal elite have been decimated by a long list of prominent figures and well known celebrities that have been accused of sexual misconduct of one sort or another. To illustrate, it's been alleged by a large number of women that famed film producer, Harvey Weinstein, sexually harassed or assaulted them. Actresses Rose McGowan and Ashley Judd are included in that group of women, according to a BBC report. Gwyneth Paltrow and Angelina Jolie also claimed they were harassed.[104]

In addition to the impact this series of sexual misconduct allegations have had on the Hollywood Left, hashtag #MeToo has sprung up into use by other women who have claimed to have experienced sexual harassment and assault.[105] The response to #MeToo has been widespread and pervasive.

The sexual misconduct outing of many of the Left's power elite has even spread to powerful and well known members of the old mainstream media and to Congress itself.

Added to all these elements of the Left's power coalition is the over-the-top bias of America's college and university's professors and administrators, and even K-12 teachers and school boards. The assault on free speech in particular on college campuses has been so egregious that it has led to many former Democrats swallowing those red pills discussed earlier.

Homeschooling and parents voting to elect more conservative school boards are two definitive responses to the Left's near ideological monopoly over American education.

Expect alumni donations to colleges and universities in general to trend lower in the future. Why? Angry, upset, and frustrated citizens as well as alumni, who are appalled with the unfairness of colleges and universities squelching of conservative thought, seek to level the playing field and maintain freedom of speech and expression on the campuses of the nation's institutions of higher education.

Of course, there are notable exceptions in higher education that are known for taking a more traditional approach to education. I believe their donations will increase over the Conservative Era, rather than decline. Examples of colleges that seek to educate their students along traditional American values and that promote freedom of speech on campus include Hillsdale College and Grove City College.

All of the above factors and more reinforce a trend toward the implosion of the Left's power coalition and its influence in American political life.

The Left's Strategy to Impeach President Trump Will Not Work

Finally, one other trend that has arisen since the election of Trump in 2016 is the Left's strategy to deny America and its voters the direct result of the 2016 presidential election, namely, Trump's election as president. The Left's strategy is simple — if you can't win the election, then impeach Trump instead.

It appears that the Trump-Russian collusion and subsequent investigation was one tactic that falls within this strategy. But, no concrete evidence or credible leaks have ever surfaced to support this claim.

As the Trump-Russian collusion tactic has failed, we have heard other tactics used to promote Trump's impeachment. For example, the "He is not fit for office" theme is another tactic. Or, "He obstructed justice by firing Comey, the former Director of the CIA" theme was a third tactic. What the Left purposely misses in that later accusation is that the president is the chief law enforcement officer in the United States; the president can have whatever opinion he wants on any case pending; and the president can fire anyone, who falls under his jurisdiction including Comey.

The bottom line is that the Left's strategy to impeach the president is a last desperate attempt to regain power that the voters have taken away from the Democratic Party and their left-wing supporters and enablers.

The Left's strategy to impeach Trump will fail. There is no Constitutional or legal basis for overturning the results of a legitimate election. From a political point of view, it is a strategic mistake with generational consequences.

The Left's strategy to impeach Trump only serves to further alienate the American people from the failed policies and programs of the Democratic Party. It is actually solidifying and strengthening Trump's close connection with the voters. It's also widening the Electoral College margin of Trump's likely 2020 reelection victory.

The Left's Strategy for One or More Government Shutdowns Will Not Work

In a desperate attempt to hold on to power, the Democratic Party might try to use a series of political issues that they refuse to budge on, in order to create one or more government shutdowns. Because past government shutdowns usually tarnished the Republican Party's national image, the Democrats are hoping one or more government shutdowns might build more support for their candidates in the upcoming Congressional elections. In their minds, government shutdowns might give them a powerful wedge issue to fight Republicans.

There are two ways this strategy might be implemented by Democrats. First, they might use a series of short government shutdowns (less than two weeks) to block several conservative legislative initiatives from getting passed into law, or alternatively, they might use these shutdowns to push several progressive socialist policies into law.

Second, this strategy might be used to create a lengthy government shutdown (more than two weeks, possibly up to two months in length) that will cause damage to the country in certain key areas of the Federal government.

The reasons for this strategy implementation are to inflict maximum damage on the American economy and on President Trump. Right now, the American economy is sailing along with robust GDP growth and incredible optimism. Unemployment is down and the stock market is up. Damaging the economy might dampen some of America's optimism and might help the Democrats regain the House of Representatives. Of course, regaining the House also means Democrats might try to impeach the president.

The American people see the Democrats as resisting President Trump and his agenda. They see the Democrats as primarily resisting not only President Trump, but also America's progress. This is a terrible approach for the Democratic Party. If they decide to follow this strategy, they will be hurting themselves even more.

The Left's strategy for one or more government shutdowns will simply not work.

With so many trends moving against the Democratic Party and so many potential Democratic Party strategies unlikely to work for them, the next question to answer is: Will the Democratic Party even survive in the future?

Chapter 6

Will the Democratic Party Survive in the Future?

With all the trends we enumerated in the last chapter, it appears that the Democratic Party is on the ropes from a political survival point of view.

Indeed, we know from the current scoreboard of political officeholders, from the White House to the House and to the Senate, from the governor's mansions to the state legislative chambers, the Conservative Era is taking hold across the nation.

In the Supreme Court, it is likely that three more seats will open in the next few years and the Senate will confirm three more Constitutional conservatives. The Senate rules are in place. Only a simple majority is needed to confirm Supreme Court Justices as well as Circuit Courts of Appeal judges and District Court judges.

As I predicted in 2015, the Supreme Court will probably see a conservative super-majority with four new Constitutional conservative justices appointed by the president in his first term of office. President Trump is also quickly filling the Circuit Courts of Appeal and District Court openings with judges that believe in the Constitution and the Rule of Law.

The trends are evident and growing stronger by the year. The Electoral College balance of power favors Heartland America over Coastal America. Small contributors favor making donations to the Republican Party rather than the Democratic Party. Identity politics is in decline with identity groups no longer as monolithic as in the past and less likely to vote with their identity groups in the future. In stark contrast, emerging tribal communities that share similar values and lifestyles are trending more conservative.

On top of that, the Left's power coalition is imploding and fragmenting, leaving their power vastly eroded. In addition, the Left's strategy to impeach President Trump is floundering without any legitimate Constitutional or legal basis. Plus, it is further alienating the Democratic Party from American voters.

What's next for the damaged Democratic Party?

Will it be a Minority Party for a Generation?

America, as we know, is a two-party system. Sometimes, one party holds a political edge for years or even decades and wins more seats on average than the other party. In these situations, we can call the dominant party that holds the electoral edge in most political contests the majority party. The other party that is less likely to win is the minority party.

Given the long-range and short-range trends in play today as well as the reality of election results from about the last decade or so, we can say that the Democratic Party might emerge as America's minority party for the next generation or two. This would roughly coincide with the duration of the new American Constitutional Era we are witnessing now, the Conservative Era.

But, actually that particular scenario might be the best case scenario for the Democratic Party among the ones we discuss in this chapter.

The only better political strategy for the Democratic Party to follow is to align itself with the more conservative views of the American electorate, views they currently reject outright. This scenario does not appear likely for the immediate future.

There are other possibilities for the Democratic Party as we will see below.

Will it Rename and Rebrand itself to be the Progressive Socialist Party?

Bernie Sanders, a self-proclaimed socialist, drew considerable attention and support during his run for the Democratic presidential nomination. That response from Democratic Party primary and caucus voters highlighted the fact that some Democratic Party members or potential members have a strong progressive socialist or outright socialist point of view.

Clearly, we know that Democratic Party voters were leery of and lacked enthusiasm for Clinton and the Democratic Party establishment. Sanders brought some dry (but unworkable and impractical) big government ideas to the campaign trail.

Instead of keeping the worn out Democratic Party name and brand, the Democratic Party might opt to rename and rebrand itself. In reality, the Democratic Party is the party of progressive socialism, democratic socialism, and socialism. Clinton even self-identified herself as a progressive.

Note how the terms Democrat and liberal are not used as often any more. This makes sense since the Democrats of old, like John F. Kennedy and Scoop Jackson, would no longer be welcome in the present day Democratic Party. The term liberal is derived from the word liberty and in a classic sense refers to open-mindedness to ideas. With the closing of the Left's minds to any ideas that differ from their own, the word liberal no longer applies to the Democratic Party.

In addition, the policies and programs of the current day Democratic Party resemble progressive ideology taken to the limit of full-blown socialism or Marxism. In fact, the present day Democratic Party with their extreme leftist elements appear to have gone a step further in trying to shut down free speech in a way that smacks of a totalitarian regime.

So, it's really not a big stretch for the Democratic Party to give up its traditional name "Democratic Party" and rename and rebrand itself more accurately to the Progressive Socialist Party. That name and brand accommodates most of its far left members. The exceptions are those on the extreme left who might prefer a one party system and totalitarian communism. Remember that communism is a form of socialism that take big government command and control to a totalitarian level. North Korea with its terrible and brutal form of authoritarian government and destitute poverty is one example of socialism run completely and pathologically amok.

Renaming and rebranding the Democratic Party is explicitly more honest with the American people than the worn out traditional name for the Democratic Party. It is progressive (meaning "progressing toward socialism"), socialist (meaning "pushing for big government control and limiting individual personal freedoms"), and it is progressive socialist (meaning "it's attempting to finish getting to socialism").

Yet, renaming and rebranding the Democratic Party to a more appropriate name and brand do not change the electoral calculus. The long-range trends and the short-range trends are still in place. The dynamic election models largely stay intact. Whatever they choose to call their party, the Democratic Party is fundamentally out of touch with the American Constitutional Era we have entered into.

To the best of our knowledge, the Conservative Era is here to stay for one or two generations. As we said earlier in this book, an American Constitutional Era lasts approximately 24 to 36 years.

The renaming and rebranding strategy of the Democratic Party to the Progressive Socialist Party is the second major scenario and strategy that might take place. Let's look at three other possible scenarios.

Will it Join Forces with the Old Mainstream Media to Form the Globalist Party?

This is an odd scenario for the Democratic Party to follow. But, nevertheless, it's a real possibility. The old mainstream media continues on its journalistic and business slide. Its credibility and believability continues to decline. The Democratic Party finds itself in a similar decline. Its credibility and financial viability are suspect in both the short-range and the long-range timeframes.

It's reasonable to consider that these comparable groups can pull off a political merger. After all, both the Democratic Party and the old mainstream media are vehemently opposed to President Trump and his current administration. It seems like they both have analogous goals and often follow parallel tactics. In the recent past, there is some evidence that the Democratic Party and old mainstream media even coordinate actions together.

In addition, we know that over the years, Democratic Party staff members will leave their political positions and take up residence in new positions in the old mainstream media. Of course, some also leave media positions to take new jobs in the Democratic Party or in politically-appointed jobs within Democratic Party administrations. The latter job-hopping to take jobs within Democratic Party administrations will be curtailed as Democratic political candidates lose elections and lose the ability to form Democratic administrations. The past revolving door between the Democratic Party and the old mainstream media is well-known.

With both organizations hurting, with the old mainstream media feeling layoffs and downsizing, with the Democratic Party political candidates losing elections, and with Democratic Party loyalists losing lucrative government staff jobs, the unemployment rate among Leftist partisans is likely going to rise further.

It might make a lot of sense for the old mainstream media and the Democratic Party to join forces and form a completely new party in which they can use their combined experience in politics and partisan news stories.

I think this new potential party might be best called the Globalist Party because it fits many of their views on world government. Of course, its political party planks would call for a United Nations led world government with America as just one of 200 or so nations led by the United Nations. Certainly, at the top of their platform would be political planks about strict climate change policies. Expect that such policies would adversely and unduly impact

America, should they ever be implemented in some highly unlikely scenario.

The European Union will likely endorse the Democratic Party's possible merger with the old mainstream media to form a Globalist Party. That, in itself, is a signal that such a Global Party would fail in elections across America.

Will it Merge with the Green Party and the Socialist Party USA to Form the Democratic Socialist Party?

A fourth scenario and strategy for the Democratic Party is to do another type of merger. In this case, the remnants of the Democratic Party can merge with both the Green Party and the Socialist Party USA to form the new Democratic Socialist Party.

Such a newly formed Democratic Socialist Party would appeal to progressives, socialists, Marxists, and environmental extremists. It might even appeal to those who believe in communism, although it will not go far enough to satisfy those who seek totalitarianism or anarchism.

In terms of political clout, a Democratic Socialist Party would likely not register much on the Richter scale. If a Trump rally measures 7.0 on a political Richter scale, a Democratic Socialist Party rally would probably be 1.0 on the same scale.

Recall with earthquake measurements that each number higher on the Richter scale represents a factor of ten times the power of the next lower number. That means, a 7.0 earthquake is ten times more powerful as a 6.0 earthquake.

Bottom line politically, the Democratic Socialist Party formed from the leftover Democratic Party as well as the Green Party, and the Socialist Party USA, would appeal to many on the Left, but it would fail as a national party. Its membership and impact on elections would be minimal. It would not be a factor at the national, state, or local levels, in general. However, it might win a few mayoral elections in coastal cities.

Will it simply shut down like the Whig Party?

Political parties reflect the will of the American voters. Throughout American History, given political parties ebb and flow. Sometimes the leadership of parties will shift, sometimes party platform planks will evolve, and sometimes support for particular policies and programs will dramatically change. Sometimes parties will change their names. Sometimes political parties die. Let's look at a few examples of political party realignments and changes.

The presidential election of 1828 was an historic and critical presidential election. Andrew Jackson won that year with 178 Electoral Votes to John Quincy Adams 83 Electoral Votes.[106] In addition to being a popular election with considerable interest and involvement of voters, it was also a critical election because there was a fundamental party realignment.

The Democrat-Republicans under Andrew Jackson with the help of Martin Van Buren and John Calhoun morphed into the Jackson Party or the "Democratic" Republican Party. Note the slight difference in name from the Democrat-Republican Party to the Democratic Republican Party, or simply, the Democratic Party. In 1832, the name Democratic Party stuck and it became the commonly used name for that party from then on.[107]

Of interest, John Quincy Adams' Democrat-Republican supporters became the "National" Republican Party. Notice how both Andrew Jackson and John Quincy Adams started with backing from the Democrat-Republicans. The critical election of 1828 also saw the formation of America's first third party, the Anti-Masonic Party that sought freedom of opportunity for individuals.[108]

By 1834, the National Republican Party had become known as the Whig Party, or simply the Whigs, when the National Republicans joined forces with the Anti-Masonic Party and others then led at the time by John Calhoun.[109]

While the Whig Party was active for a number of presidential elections, it eventually died out during the 1856 presidential election. James Buchanan (Democratic Party) was elected president that year with 174 Electoral Votes to John C. Fremont's

(Republican Party) 114 Electoral Votes and Millard Fillmore's (American Party) 8 Electoral Votes.[110]

The Whig Party's fifth and final national convention was held in September 1856. At that convention, the Whig's unanimously endorsed the American Party presidential candidate, Millard Fillmore. The Whig Party went into the history books.[111]

Another scenario and strategy for the Democratic Party to follow in their current situation is to simply shut down the Democratic Party and close their books on a party in precipitous decline. Many parties have adopted such a strategy including the Whig Party cited above, the American Party, the Liberty Party, and the Constitutional Union Party.

This is a real possibility. The decision might be heavily influenced by the actions of the Republican Party with regard to their future political party realignment.

Will the Democratic Party ever elect another president?

Let's summarize the five likely strategies and scenarios for the Democratic Party:

- Become a minority party for a generation
- Rename and rebrand itself to the Progressive Socialist Party
- Join forces with the old mainstream media to form the Globalist Party
- Merge with the Green Party and the Socialist Party USA to form the Democratic Socialist Party
- Shut down like the Whig Party

Given those five paths the Democratic Party might choose to follow, I predict the Democratic Party will not elect another president in the Conservative Era, approximately the next 24 – 36 years. If the Democratic Party is still active in one or two generations, and if they align themselves with the will of the voters, it's possible they might have a resurgence. But, given their current strategies and tactics as well as their present day policies and programs, I think it is unlikely.

Prediction #1 – The Future of the Democratic Party

I predict the Democratic Party will shut down as a major political party in the United States.

I believe some progressives within the Democratic Party will link up with progressives and RINOs (Republicans In Name Only) from the Republican Party that have decided to form a new party, the Republican Progressive Party. The Republican Progressive Party, as we discuss later, will be a minority party.

I believe other progressives within the Democratic Party will join either the Green Party or the Socialist Party USA, depending on their respective policy preferences.

I believe many downsized old mainstream media staff will also join the newly formed Republican Progressive Party.

I think the Democratic Party changes will take place in the next two to six year timeframe.

Although this is a relatively short-range forecast, it is based on both long-range and short-range analysis. If a strong, determined, and articulate leader or leadership team emerges in the next few years, the future of the Democratic Party might take a significantly different path. But, as it stands today, I expect the Democratic Party to shut down in the near future.

Let's move now from the Democratic Party to the Republican Party and look at its likely future.

Chapter 7

What Will Happen to the Republican Party in the Future?

In contrast to the Democratic Party that is facing serious issues that make its survival unlikely, the Republican Party is embroiled in a political battle for its heart, soul, and mind. One wing of the Republican Party is more conservative, the other faction is more progressive. How are the battle lines drawn?

The Battle for Control of the Republican Party

The conservative portion of the Republican Party strongly adheres to the principles of the Founding Fathers. They believe in the Constitution and the Rule of Law applied equally to all, including those serving within the government itself. They advocate for morality throughout government, the elimination of corruption and crony capitalism, and freedom for all American citizens. They believe strongly in the Bill of Rights.

The conservative portion of the Republican Party believes in **American Exceptionalism**. They believe that America's truth began with the exceptional idea that God is the "Author of our Liberty," that liberty was given by God to the people, and then was loaned by the people to its elected representatives for limited purposes, for a limited time, when the representatives served the people faithfully and morally.

Conservatives promote a strong national defense for America and principled American leadership on the world stage. They support law and order within America. They also support America's law enforcement officers, who defend our peace and safety at home.

In the economy, conservatives stand for pro-growth tax policies, spending policies, regulatory policies, and monetary policies. In a nutshell, that means conservatives fight for lower taxes, necessary (but not wasteful) government spending, minimal regulations (with a few exceptions for health, safety, and other essential priorities), and a monetary policy that is steady and includes a strong dollar and keeping inflation in check.

The other wing of the Republican Party is more progressive in their thinking. In this sense, they are similar to the Democratic Party. They see a greater role for government than conservatives. They are comfortable with keeping taxes much higher than conservatives, with spending more for additional government programs than is strictly necessary, with permitting greater deficits and higher national debt, allowing more regulations whose impact is to throttle back economic activity, and with easier monetary policy. They are more apt to go along with a weaker dollar and higher inflation (manifest on either a short-range or long-range basis).

Sometimes conservatives refer to the other wing of the Republican Party as Establishment Republicans or RINOs (Republicans-In-Name-Only, as we mentioned earlier). If you study the history of American political parties, or are a part of the baby boom generation, you might recall the 1964 presidential election when Barry Goldwater (a conservative) fought Nelson Rockefeller (a liberal) for the Republican presidential nomination. At the time, conservatives referred to the more liberal Republicans as part of the Eastern Liberal Establishment.

Obviously, the split within the Republican Party has been palpable and evident for quite some time. Today, the conservative wing of the Republican Party is in a near stand-off battle with the progressive wing of the Republican Party.

The battle almost seems like two tectonic plates caught in a collision between two continents. Eventually, the collision causes the continental crusts to buckle forming a new mountain range.[112] A new political party might be the result of this on-going political collision.

The questions we need to address are:

- What possible strategies can the Republican Party follow to resolve this problem?
- What potential scenarios might we envision that can end this political stalemate in the Republican Party, and give the American voters the results they expect from Washington?
- Finally, what will happen to the Republican Party in the future?

Will it Pass More Conservative Legislation?

Voters have been signaling for about a decade that they want an end to the progressive socialist agenda offered by the Democratic Party. In addition, voters have also been flashing signs that they seek more conservative policy prescriptions for the nation.

To illustrate, the historic 63-seat turnover in House seats from the Democratic Party to the Republican Party in November 2010 was a direct result of the electorate's dismay with the Democratic Party passing the Affordable Care Act (ACA) in March 2010 and President Obama's follow-up signature on that legislation. Recall the ACA was approved by Congress without a single Republican Party vote. The Democratic Party subsequently paid a heavy price for the ACA passage with the dramatic loss of the House just eight months later.

Along with the battle for the control of the Republican Party within the party itself is another battle between both parties and the American people. American voters are demanding more conservative action from their representatives and senators in the House and Senate.

President Trump was elected with a specific policy agenda and concrete solutions in mind. While the president has carried forward on that agenda on his own with Executive Orders where possible, Trump's agenda that require legislative involvement have largely been stymied in Congress, despite Republican Party control of both the House and Senate.

It seems that no longer is single-party control of the White House, Senate, and House sufficient to guarantee legislative action. American voters who gladly gave the Republican Party such single-party control expected more from the Republican Party. They expected dramatic action quickly.

To illustrate, one theme was heard over-and-over again throughout the 2016 presidential election campaign: "Repeal and Replace Obamacare." Sometimes that theme was even more specific: "Repeal and Replace Obamacare on Day One." We heard these themes repeatedly.

One possible strategy for members of the Republican Party in the House and the Senate to follow is to jump on the Trump train and pass more conservative legislation. Instead of joining the Democratic Party resistance movement attempting to thwart the president as some Republicans seem to have done, they should adopt, defend, and promote the Trump agenda. After all, President Trump was elected president on that agenda.

Incidentally, a number of Trump's election promises were mirrored by Congressional Republicans during their own election and reelection campaigns. Certainly, Republicans keeping their own promises to the American voters is a solid reason for conservative action as well.

Many Republicans in the House and Senate were elected to office to accomplish these legislative tasks:

- Repeal and replace Obamacare
- Cut taxes on individuals
- Cut taxes on corporations to bring jobs back home
- Slash regulations to spur on the economy and create new jobs
- Control and contain out-of-control government spending

- Rein in skyrocketing government deficits
- Limit national debt
- Protect our borders with tougher immigration laws and by building a fence

I think the Republican Party will not get many more chances to deliver results that American voters are demanding. If the Republican Party fails to act on what voters are demanding, they will see a significant political party realignment of their own.

One strategy and scenario for the future of the Republican Party is to pass more conservative legislation, along the lines that President Trump and many Republicans were elected on. If it does, the GOP will stay together as a party, albeit divided and somewhat contentious. Time is running out for the Republican Party as it currently exists. Conservative action is needed right away.

Will it be Forced to become More Conservative by Voters?

If the Republican Party continues to block President Trump and his agenda, the American voters will not switch to voting for Democratic Congressional candidates (unless they run as true conservatives). Expect to see a different approach by the electorate next.

In this circumstance, I think many Republican voters will support more conservative Republican candidates in primaries. Rather than voting for Democratic candidates, I think their preferred approach will be to force the Republican Party to become more conservative by electing more conservative candidates to run for office.

Another thing will happen too. Some Establishment Republicans will read the polls and will opt out of running for their own nominations for reelection in cases where the primary challengers are conservative and look particularly strong. As examples, consider Sen. Bob Corker of Tennessee and Sen. Jeff Flake of Arizona. Both decided not to seek reelection, probably because they believed they would lose. They thought they faced more conservative electorates in their respective states.

In addition to this method of building a more conservative Republican Party, American voters are likely to elect more conservative Republicans running against incumbent Democratic Party officeholders. In the Senate there are nearly 50 Democratic senators. Some of them will be replaced with conservative Republican challengers in a further effort to turn America back to its more conservative principles and roots.

Let's summarize this second scenario dealing with the Republican Party's future.

In this scenario, voters not satisfied with the Republican Party (because it often operates as a roadblock to Trump's agenda) simply choose more conservative primary challengers over incumbent Establishment Republicans and RINOs. In addition, it votes incumbent Establishment Democrats out-of-office during general elections as well. This results in additional conservative Republicans in office.

The bottom line, as I like to say, is that in this scenario the Republican Party is forced to become more conservative and thus, more responsive to the American people.

What are some other options for the Republican Party?

Will it Morph into a New Majority Party – the Conservative Party?

A third possibility for the Republican Party is to recognize our new American Constitutional Era, the Conservative Era, in American History. With that recognition, the Republican Party can morph itself into the Conservative Party that the American people are seeking.

It would, of course, require a name change and some work on policies and solutions. It would also necessitate some organizational, management, and personnel changes going from the Republican National Committee to the Conservative National

Committee. Leaders and officeholders would need to accept the reasons for the significant changes and either commit to the changes or bow out gracefully, possibly to retire to the private sector.

In a similar vein, the state party structure of the Republican Party in each state would need to reflect the national level changes. The state party organizations would need to follow all existing state election laws regarding such a major change.

All told this strategy requires a lot of work and effort, but it does cement the Conservative Party's future role in American politics for at least 24 – 36 years.

It also would bring an end to the anger and frustration that voters have for the two major parties that have been largely unresponsive to their desires for a return to conservative principles and policies.

Of course, some current Republican Party leaders and officeholders will stringently object to a new Conservative Party coming out of the existing Republican Party. That's why there is still another fourth related scenario that I foresee. It might take place instead with a slightly higher probability.

Will it Split into Two New Parties – Conservative Party and Republican Progressive Party?

The fourth strategy and scenario for the future of the Republican Party is for the two wings of the fractious Republican Party – the conservative wing and the progressive wing – to split the current Republican Party into two distinct new parties.

Out of this historic political party realignment, America would have a Conservative Party and a Republican Progressive Party. Other names for the new parties are possible as well. Consider for example these ten potential names (the list includes my original two suggested names for completeness):

- Conservative Party
- Conservative Renaissance Party
- Conservative American Party
- American Conservative Party
- Conservative Constitutional Party
- Make America Great Again Party
- Republican Progressive Party
- Republican-Democratic Party (similar to the 1828 party name change, but in reverse)
- Republican-Democratic Progressive Party
- Progressive Party

Given the needs of American voters, the Conservative Party would likely become the majority party in America during the Conservative Era. The Republican Progressive Party would then likely become the minority party. In this scenario, I assume the Democratic Party would cease to exist. Their members would scatter and most would likely join the Republican Progressive Party, the Green Party, and the Socialist Party USA. Some might even turn to the Conservative Party because they prefer supporting a party in power where they can maintain some level of personal involvement and potential influence.

Will the Republican Party or the Conservative Party become the Majority Party for a Generation?

Clearly, the Democratic Party has lost the support of American voters throughout most of America, as evidenced by their across-the-board loss of elections and offices held. These days the Democratic Party is best able to obtain election victories in solidly blue states and largely blue cities, both generally located on America's coastlines. There are some limited exceptions.

The American voter is expressing a strong preference for the traditional conservative principles of morality, freedom, peace, and prosperity. The American voter is also showing its ardent resolve to elect conservative political candidates that not only will "talk the talk" during a political campaign, but will actually "walk the walk" when elected to office.

During the ensuing Conservative Era, the majority party in America will depend heavily on the actual future of the Republican Party.

If the Republican Party immediately embarks on adopting, defending, and promoting more conservative legislation, the Republican Party will become the majority party.

If, on the other hand, the Republican Party continues to engage in internal battles among the conservative wing and the progressive wing and legislative gridlock continues unabated, expect the second scenario discussed above as a real possibility. In this instance, the voters force the reluctant Republican Party to become more conservative with conservative primary challengers to Establishment Republicans and RINOs. In addition, the voters will replace existing Establishment Democrats with conservative Republicans in general election battles. In this second scenario, the Republican Party will also become the majority party for one or two generations.

If the Republican Party morphs into the Conservative Party, it's a political slam-dunk. The Conservative Party will become the majority party.

In the final scenario in which the Republican Party splits into the Conservative Party and the Republican Progressive Party, the Conservative Party will likely become the majority party during the Conservative Era.

Prediction #2 – The Future of the Republican Party

While many observers and political pundits might expect the Republican Party to map their own future and control their own destiny, my sense is that power is a political aphrodisiac and it blinds otherwise intelligent and rationale politicians from taking the best course of action.

I predict the following with regard to the future of the Republican Party. It will have limited success in supporting the Trump agenda because the internal battle for control of the Republican Party will continue between the conservative wing and progressive wings of the party.

During the prelude to the upcoming Congressional elections, I expect conservatives to challenge Establishment Republicans and RINOs in many primary elections and win. I also expect many conservatives to wage strong campaigns against incumbent Democratic officeholders and be victorious in many general election battles. I predict this short-range trend will continue for several more Congressional election cycles.

However, I do not believe that the voters will achieve their goal of changing the Republican Party anytime soon. There are too many incumbents and too many advantages for those in power for the voters to move an entire party quickly.

With regard to the Republican Party morphing into the Conservative Party, I think the pushback from the progressive wing would be formidable and unlikely to take place.

I predict the most likely scenario is that the battle for control of the Republican Party will become more intense and the party will fragment into two new parties, the Conservative Party and the Republican Progressive Party. Further, I predict the Conservative Party will become the likely majority party and the Republican Progressive Party will become the loyal opposition and minority party.

Again, I expect these two parties will maintain their balance of power throughout the Conservative Era which will probably last about 24 – 36 years, approximately one to two generations.
With an understanding of the potential political party realignments that appear likely to take place in America, let's turn our attention next to what will happen with political issues in America in the future.

Part III

What Will Happen with America's Top Political Issues in the Future?

Chapter 8

What Will Happen with Obamacare and How Will Conservatives Move Forward?

In many ways, the impetus for the historic and critical 2016 presidential election were some major political issues that were debated during the presidential election and since that election, but are not yet fully resolved. We might say charitably that these important American political issues are still "in process." In other words, they are yet to be settled. This is the case, despite the fact that many Americans and their representatives are debating these issues and are working hard to resolve them as quickly as possible.

Let's take a quick tour of many of the most contentious issues of our time and attempt to predict how they will be handled by our political system in the near future. Note that American voters might not always get what they want in the short-run. But, in the long-run, they have a much better opportunity to achieve precisely what they seek. Elections clearly have consequences and the American people are rejecting the failed progressive socialist policies of the past and are replacing them with conservative principles in the new Conservative Era.

Let's start with an issue that came up frequently in the 2016 presidential election, was hotly debated in Congress in 2017, and has yet to be fully addressed.

Will America Repeal and Replace Obamacare?

A Martian that wanted to learn about Earth elections and dutifully sat through numerous presidential debates, campaign speeches, and political rallies in 2016 might have guessed that Obamacare (whatever that meant to a visiting Martian) would have been systematically repealed and totally replaced a few days after our new president was sworn into office. Why? One of the most popular and frequently heard campaign themes of the 2016 presidential election was "Repeal and Replace Obamacare." It was articulated often by various Republican presidential contenders and by the eventual Republican presidential candidate himself.

However, as anyone who follows major political issues in the U. S. knows, once the new president took office, repeal and replace Obamacare became a Herculean task. The Democratic Party stood steadfastly and monolithically against any attempt to take down President Obama's signature entitlement program that they had hoped would eventually lead to a full-blown, single-payer, socialist healthcare system for America.

On the other side of the political aisle, Republican House and Senate members disagreed on how best to repeal and replace Obamacare. Some were fearful that some changes in Obamacare would lead to more uninsured Americans. Democrats apparently were skilled in raising worry among its constituents about loss of benefits.

Other Republicans faced concerned groups of citizens in vociferous Town Hall meetings. Still other Republicans feared that an outright repeal of Obamacare without a corresponding replacement alternative would be difficult for states and citizens to absorb financially. The fact that Obamacare was on the verge of utter and complete bankruptcy was not a sufficient motivation to put Obamacare out of its steady decline and progressive misery.

Fear won out over reason. Republicans were afraid to get rid of Obamacare. Democrats were afraid to allow consumers the freedom to manage a free market in healthcare. Most economic analysts that sought a smooth-running, reasonably-priced healthcare industry realized Obamacare was poor legislation.

Further, they saw the ACA law had yielded a woefully inadequate system that was lingering close to bankruptcy.

What Four Actions Will Conservatives Take to Move Forward?

Truly, conservatives faced with repealing and replacing Obamacare need to take four specific actions. These actions can effectively apply as a working strategy to other legislative tasks they face as well. Count on conservatives taking these four actions to enhance their political bargaining power to achieve legislative goals. Other Republicans might reluctantly follow the lead of conservatives, if they choose to increase their chances of staying in office.

First, conservatives will learn to ignore the noise coming from the Left. They will recognize that conservative voters do not constitute a vocal constituent group. The silent majority is still silent and is still a majority.

The noise conservative Republicans and Establishment Republicans hear from the Left is loud and annoying, but it's also shallow, hollow, and it's not representative of the entire population. The Left's polls, apparently often used to foster and support their leftwing positions, are notoriously inaccurate as well. Why take all of these polls so seriously?

Plain and simple, the Left is in the business of political activism – namely, moving our nation toward progressive socialism and ultimately, to outright democratic socialism as many Leftists call it. Conservative voters, in sharp contrast, are in the business of living life – specifically, they seek life, liberty, and the pursuit of happiness, for themselves and their families.

Conservatives don't seek a detailed involvement in, or an intimate working relationship with, their government. It takes valuable time away from conservatives, who prefer pursuing interests other than enlarging the size and scope of government as progressives wish.

Conservative Republicans will, and Establishment Republicans need, to ignore:

- Vocal special interest groups, clamoring for bigger government expenditures that bankrupt the nation's treasury and that saddle our children with mountains of national debt
- Powerful leftwing lobbying groups
- Wealthy progressive and socialist political donors and the noisy groups they fund
- The old mainstream media
- The old mainstream media's constant barrage of socialist narratives and fake news stories
- The Left's inaccurate polls
- Those who promote inaccurate and static economic models, misleading Congressional legislators with unrealistic numbers

Second, conservatives will sharpen their skills and will come to fully understand the principles they believe in, and advocate for, in the marketplace of ideas. There is a huge difference between free market capitalism and big government, bureaucratic, and democratic socialism. Free market capitalism consists of freedom and free markets, not the crony capitalism that sometimes sticks up its ugly head with powerful government agencies favoring selected companies or industries.

Government should not be in the business of picking winners and losers in a free market economy. Winners and losers are chosen by consumers, voting with their wallets. I'm sorry for any unemployed Leftists, but social engineers touting progressive policies and socialist programs need not apply for jobs in a free market economy.

Sometimes, it seems like many Establishment Republicans like to use the words of conservatives too loosely. Sure, it is true that such conservative words and themes test well in polls (at least those polls that are accurate). But, have these same Establishment Republicans taken the time to understand the conservative principles they espouse to the electorate and understand why those principles work consistently throughout an economy and a free nation?

If conservative Republicans and Establishment Republicans fully understand the principles they articulate in campaigns, an important benefit is they can accomplish their next action item.

Third, Republicans of all types will express their conservative principles to Americans. They need to vigorously debate their opponents and not continually stand down in the face of disagreeable and emotional political adversaries. They need to increase support for conservative principles, policies, and programs among the electorate. They need to pick up support from those who have been persuaded falsely that democratic socialism is better than freedom, free enterprise, free markets, and capitalism.

In a sobering poll (that we can all hope is inaccurate), 58% of American millennials would prefer to live under socialism, communism, or fascism. Only 42% favored capitalism.[113] That's a sad commentary on America's educational system and its effectiveness.

It appears that America's K-12 system as well as America's colleges and universities are not adequately educating younger Americans on the benefits of freedom, free enterprise, free markets, and capitalism. That's one more reason why Republican political candidates and officeholders need to take the political debate over political ideology to all Americans.

Fourth, conservative Republicans and Establishment Republicans will argue for and will pass legislation that is based on sound conservative principles. These legislative accomplishments will help the nation to grow and to succeed, to thrive and to prosper, and to live in peace with security at home and abroad.

In other words, conservative Republicans and Establishment Republicans first consideration in office should not be fundraising for the next election cycle or even winning ever again. It should be what's best for America now and in the future. Conservatives seek what's best for America.

The 2 + 2 Voluntary Term Limitation Pledge – No More than Two Terms and Two Offices

Incidentally, it's my view, that conservative politicians (and actually all politicians) should view government as a temporary civic duty. You serve no more than two terms in any one government elected office. You serve in no more than two different government offices over your entire lifetime. Then, you return to the private sector.

I believe that voluntarily limiting government service to two terms in office and two offices in a lifetime would keep officeholders focused on service, not on job security for life. I also think it would help to eliminate corruption. In my opinion, the more time spent in office and the more power of that office, the more likely an officeholder can and will become corrupted in office. Of course, this rule of thumb doesn't fit many moral and ethical individuals, who run for office with a deep sense of duty and service.

To illustrate, with this 2 + 2 limitation approach, someone can run for the U. S. House and serve two terms in the House. Then, run for a U. S. Senate seat and serve two more terms in the Senate. Then, after those 16 years of government service, that person can return to the private sector.

Another example might be a citizen, who serves two terms as a governor and then two terms as president. Again, that amounts to 16 years of government service.

Let's return to the question of whether or not we will repeal and replace Obamacare.

Prediction #3 – The Future of American Healthcare

Republicans need to pass legislation that rolls back previous bad laws like Obamacare and that replaces those bad laws with legislation that empowers pro-economic growth policies. New laws when appropriate should also provide a safety net for those genuinely requiring help in our society.

I predict with all the inherent problems in the current Obamacare law, it will be completely repealed in two to four stages within a few years. The reason for the obvious delay is the lack of conservative Republican votes in Congress for a complete repeal immediately.

Fortunately, the first stage in repealing the Obamacare law has already taken place with the elimination of the Obamacare individual mandate tax penalty in the Tax Cuts and Jobs Act discussed in the next chapter.

In addition, I predict that in parallel with the multi-stage Obamacare repeal will be a concurrent multi-stage implementation of free market reforms in its place that will significantly drive down healthcare premiums, co-payments, and deductibles.

Competition within a free market always tends to minimize the cost to consumers of products and services, while maximizing innovation and productivity, and optimizing the use of scarce resources within a free economy and free nation.

The free market reforms will also be supplemented by a healthcare safety net for the truly needy. The safety net will likely be built on the existing Medicare structure with more freedom and leeway given to the states to meet the unique medical requirements of each state.

Funding for the new free market based, American healthcare system will be much easier to accomplish in the next few years rather than in the past 2017 timeframe when the previous major repeal and replace effort took place and failed. The reason why funding will be easier in the next few years will be the continuing growth of GDP (and consequently, the growth in government revenue). Plus, after the upcoming Congressional elections, there will be more conservatives in the House and Senate. Expect the economy to be humming along in the 4.2% GDP growth range at that time as well.

Let's turn from the American healthcare system to other important political issues we face today, starting with economic growth.

Chapter 9

What Will Happen with the American Economy?

In recent years, the American economy has been in the doldrums as a result of policies that did not promote or foster economic growth. In fact, those policies probably restrained economic growth considerably. Gross Domestic Product (GDP), for example, had been lackluster, drifting along at a meager 1.9% in the fourth quarter of 2016.[114]

The day after Trump won the presidential election, New York Times columnist Paul Krugman wrote: "The economic fallout of a Donald Trump presidency will probably be severe and widespread enough to plunge the world into recession." He also wrote: "So we are very probably looking at a global recession, with no end in sight."[115]

Rather than a global recession, we are witnessing a Trump boom instead. Since the presidential election, optimism has returned to the American economy.

Real GDP growth in the third quarter of 2017 accelerated to about 3.2%,[116] with some growth forecasts for 2018 in the 4% range. The Dow Jones hit the 25,000 milestone the first week of January in 2018 and 26,000 milestone about two weeks later. The 25,000 milestone represents a staggering 7,000 point rise or a 36% increase in value since President Trump was elected. Unemployment is at a 17 year low as well.[117] The economic outlook is consistent and positive.

Let's consider what's next with the American economy.

Will America Go with a Comprehensive Pro-Growth Economic Plan?

In December 2017, the House and Senate debated and passed a tax cut plan that goes a considerable distance toward a comprehensive pro-growth economic plan. A complete pro-growth economic plan requires pro-growth tax policies, spending policies, regulatory policies, and monetary policies.

The Tax Cuts and Jobs Act[118] includes the following key provisions for individuals and families:

- Increases the standard deduction for single taxpayers from $6,500 to $12,000 and for married taxpayers from $13,000 to $24,000
- Permits the deduction of state and local income, property, and sales taxes up to a $10,000 limit
- Increases the child tax credit from $1,000 to $2,000
- Keeps the mortgage interest deduction for existing mortgages
- Eliminates the Obamacare individual mandate tax penalty

The Tax Cuts and Jobs Act[119] also includes these components and features for job creators:

- Lowers the corporate tax rate from its previous high rate of 35% in 2017 down to 21% effective January 1, 2018
- Permits immediate full-cost write-offs for new equipment for enhancements to operations for businesses
- Preserves the Research and Development (R&D) tax credit to encourage "Made in America" innovations for both products and services
- Preserves the low income housing tax credit to help create affordable housing
- Eliminates incentives for corporations to move jobs, headquarters, and research overseas

Note that the incredibly high corporate tax rate of 35% was the highest corporate tax rate in the industrialized world before this tax cut. That high tax rate was a substantial speed bump on our economy's economic growth.

The reduction of the corporate tax rate to 21% will lead to considerable future growth in jobs, the economy, and even tax revenues. That might be a surprise to some people who think a tax rate decrease automatically leads to lower tax revenue. In modeling, we call that kind of thinking (or model) a static model. It doesn't allow for the dynamic nature of the economy to kick in and impact other variables in the economy.

In the case of the Tax Cuts and Jobs Act, you can expect that tax revenues will actually increase because overall revenues will be higher. Why? A smaller percentage of a higher number can yield much higher total tax revenues, as we have learned from other major tax cuts in America's history.

To illustrate, suppose a 35% corporate tax rate brings in $350 of tax revenue from $1,000 of corporate income (35% of $1,000 = $350). If we lower the corporate tax rate to 21%, we can expect corporations will make decisions that are in their best interest because they get to keep more money from their income.

Let's say their efforts produce a higher income of $3,000. With a 21% corporate tax rate, their tax will be $630 (21% of $3,000 = $630). Government income in the form of tax revenues will increase from the original $350 to $630. So, a tax rate cut surprisingly (to some people) will increase tax revenues.

This simple example illustrates why so many economists argue for true dynamic modeling, not static modeling when scoring legislative initiatives before voting. The key to modeling is to use models that are accurate in the real world. Dynamic models are better than static models in this case.

In addition to the above benefits for the economy, the Tax Cuts and Jobs Act also opens up the Arctic National Wildlife Refuge (ANWR) for responsible energy exploration. This feature means more energy-related jobs in Alaska and throughout the energy supply chain. It also means an estimated $1 Billion in additional tax revenues from oil revenues over a ten year period. Plus, ANWR exploration enhances America's energy independence and security.[120]

Certainly, this is a great step forward toward a comprehensive pro-growth economic plan. Additional pro-growth tax policies can be implemented in a follow-up legislative package in about two to four years as understanding and support for pro-growth economic policies gain traction and support in a more conservative Congress.

One such provision will likely be to have fewer individual income tax brackets with lower tax rates. That will further boost GDP in the coming years beyond the current pro-growth trajectory.

Let's discuss another political issue America faces today.

Will America Continue to Slash Regulations to Spur Economic Growth?

According to the Competitive Enterprise Institute, America's regulatory costs of $1.9 Trillion represent approximately 10% of the nation's GDP.[121] That's a staggering boat anchor holding back our economy. In effect, it's a 10% tax on the entire economy. That 10% regulatory cost could be invested in new innovations, new productivity boosters, new businesses, new products, new services, and of vital importance, new jobs.

While some regulations are beneficial to the economy (for example, those that promote public safety), many in my opinion are just plain silly and a waste of money. I have documented some questionable regulations in my previous books.

President Trump is on record with his intention to unburden the American people and the American economy from wasteful regulations: "Any regulation that is outdated, unnecessary, bad for workers, or contrary to the national interest will be scrapped."[122]

Toward that end, President Trump has already used the Congressional Review Act to eliminate a number of job-killing regulations.[123] The Congressional Review Act was passed by Congress as part of the 1996 Contract with America. It's a little used law that allows Congress to nullify regulations it doesn't like, subject to the president's signature.[124] With a Republican Congress and a Republican president vowing to eliminate unnecessary regulations, it will probably get to be a handy tool to cut the regulatory state.

In an Executive Order on January 30, 2017, President Trump ordered Federal agencies to identify at least two existing regulations to be eliminated for every one new regulation issued.[125] According to the White House, at the end of Fiscal Year '17, the government had actually achieved a ratio of about 22 regulations eliminated to one new regulation created. While this accomplishment is admirable and the Fiscal Year '18 plan looks aggressive, a lot more work needs to be done to empower our economy.[126]

It appears that America will continue to slash needless and wasteful regulations to create more jobs and spur further economic growth.

Another political issue hotly debated in recent years is the role of the government in holding down Federal budget deficits and restraining national debt. How will this issue play out in the coming years in the new Conservative Era?

Will America Rein in Skyrocketing Government Deficits and Limit National Debt?

As you are probably aware, many so-called deficit hawks (who are often deficit hawks only when a tax cut is on the table) criticized the Tax Cuts and Jobs Act for cutting taxes by $1.5 Trillion over the next decade. That's a common type of refrain from progressives and socialists.

It turns out, of course, that progressives and socialists are fine with increasing government spending on anything, but defense spending. In their view, such government spending is important and essential. Raising the national debt limit to accommodate such expenditures is completely justified in their view.

However, when conservatives want to give the American people tax cuts, progressives and socialists see tax cuts as reckless, gifts to the wealthy, and a tremendous liability to the economy, due to government deficits and increases in the national debt. Note that even if the tax cuts are virtually across the board, they still believe that tax cuts are for the wealthy. They don't see the benefit in giving the wealthy some of their taxes back, even though those taxes might be invested in the economy or spent for consumer needs.

The "static" analysis of progressives and socialists essentially treats a tax cut as an automatic deficit increase and a near-simultaneous increase in the national debt.

Fortunately, just as models can be used to improve polling results and to separately forecast presidential elections more accurately, models can also be effectively applied to economics. Specifically, rather than misleading legislators with static models that take into account only some variables in the economy and their direct, rigid economic impacts, dynamic models can be used to forecast the dynamic interactions of additional relevant factors and do so in such a way that generates a more accurate picture of the economy.

Rather than yielding greater Federal deficits and the need to increase the national debt further, pro-growth economic policies will likely result in greater Federal revenues and a dramatic halt to the necessity for continually increasing the national debt.

During the new Conservative Era, we can expect significant growth in our economy, as well as sustained and substantial growth in GDP. This, in turn, will lead to declining budget deficits and eventually to budget surpluses. The national debt will be capped and future growth will begin to be tackled, and then in time, reduced.

We can expect that the decades-old problem of America reining in skyrocketing Federal deficits and containing the national debt will finally be achieved through the principles and implementation of pro-growth economic policies.

Risks to the American Economy

While the economic outlook is outstanding, there are some risks with maintaining continued economic growth. First, it's important to maintain a stable monetary policy. This means our economy needs both a stable money supply and a stable value for the dollar. To tamper with the quantity of money or the value of that money throws a monkey wrench into the pricing mechanisms across the economy. A free market or even a substantially free market requires a stable monetary supply to facilitate economic transactions. Rampant inflation must be avoided.

By the way, an easy way to think about a stable money supply is with this simple example. Suppose you have a very small economy with only one product and only $100 in cash. Let's further assume the product is valued at the total of all cash in that economy, namely, $100.

If you then increase the money supply from $100 to $200 in that economy, it will take $200 to buy that same product. In effect, the dollar dropped 50% in value. It takes twice as many dollars to buy the same product. When this happens across an entire economy, dollars are worth less. We call this situation inflation.

President Trump needs to appoint people to the Federal Reserve, who recognize the need for both a stable money supply and for keeping the dollar at a stable value to promote economic growth. It's vital for a pro-growth economic plan to maintain both a stable money supply and a stable value for the dollar.

The second risk to the America economy is related to war and peace. If a war breaks out with North Korea or possibly in the Middle East, it can have a significant effect on the American economy. Wars can disrupt an economy in major ways. It is difficult to fully understand the impacts of such catastrophic events on an economy before they actually take place.

The possibility of inflation or war or any other major, unexpected event can damage our excellent economic picture.

Prediction #4 – The Future of the American Economy

Despite the risks inherent in any economy, I predict the American economy will grow in the 3.5% to 4.5% in the next several years. The foundations of a pro-growth economic plan are in place. Expect continued work on:

- Pro-Growth Tax Policies – including additional enhancement to the Tax Cuts and Jobs Act,
- Pro-Growth Spending Policies – including cuts in obviously wasteful government programs,
- Pro-Growth Regulatory Policies – including the elimination of many non-safety related and nonessential regulations, and
- Pro-Growth Monetary Policies – including those that maintain a stable money supply and a stable value of the dollar.

I predict a robust economy moving forward.

Let's turn our attention next to two more perennial political issues America has debated in recent years, illegal immigration and a secure border fence. We can also consider an additional closely-related and highly-political issue, sanctuary cities.

Chapter 10

What Will Happen with Immigration and Related Issues?

Immigration, both legal and illegal immigration, poses a myriad of political issues for America. These issues run the gamut from whether or not our current immigration laws make sense in today's world of terrorism, to whether or not we need to better enforce our existing immigration laws.

On top of those issues, we need to decide the appropriate way to handle illegal immigrants, who continue to stream across our borders. Plus, we need to deal with the illegal immigrants, who have previously come into America by surreptitious means, and also those immigrants that entered legally, but have overstayed their visa limitations.

A special concern related to illegal immigration is those cities who chose to ignore Federal law and who chose to provide sanctuary for illegal immigrants, even when some of these illegal immigrants have been convicted of felonies. Sanctuary cities have generated considerable controversy and have been widely criticized by conservatives for placing their citizens at risk by harboring known criminals.

Let's consider all these immigration related issues now.

Will We Protect Our National Security with Tougher Immigration Laws and Better Enforcement?

Illegal immigration is a particularly challenging issue because it is viewed in so many different ways by so many different people. For example, for some people, illegal immigration is thought to be an economic issue. For those Americans who see this issue as primarily an economic issue, some voters think illegal immigration means fewer jobs with lower wages for American citizens or others living legally within the United States.

On the other hand, other Americans see illegal immigration has a means for supplying the nation with an inexpensive source of labor. They also say that illegal immigrants can do jobs that American citizens reject outright.

In another variation of the economic issue, some Americans think that legal immigration (not illegal immigration) should continue, but with permission to enter America determined strictly on a merit-based system. In this case, highly trained professionals such as doctors, engineers, and software developers would be permitted to enter the nation, while those with fewer skills and education would be denied entry.

In addition to an economic issue, illegal immigration can also be a political issue. Leftists often claim it's a civil rights issue. They believe that once inside America, illegal immigrants should be accorded a certain level of civil rights. They believe that they should be given the same welfare benefits normally reserved for citizens including food, housing, medical care, and educational benefits at colleges and universities.

Surprisingly, some Leftists even argue that illegal immigrants should be given the right to vote because they live in a given city and deserve to participate in the life of the city.

Leftists go so far as saying that Americans who beleive in enforcing immigration laws and who oppose illegal immigration are actually promoting hate. It is truly an odd political position for Leftists to take. How can Americans that want the current immigration laws on the books enforced equally for all those that break those laws be hateful people? If American immigration laws are hateful, why haven't the Leftists been able to remove them from the books?

Indeed, Leftists don't have the support of most Americans on the illegal immigration issue as well as on many other issues of the day.

In sharp contrast, many conservatives think that illegal immigration is not a civil rights issue at all, but rather a desperate attempt by the progressives and socialists to hold onto political power. In the view of many conservatives, illegal immigration provides the Left with an ongoing source of potential new voters.

In particular, this is a voting bloc thought to be largely uneducated and clearly in need of government welfare programs for basic survival and long run support. Hence, this new voting bloc will probably vote for progressive socialists, who will in turn promote bigger government and larger welfare programs.

Conservatives decry the current high cost of welfare programs for illegal immigrants. Indeed, this cost is thought to range in the billions of dollars annually. In addition, there is also the considerable cost to America's judicial system for law enforcement activities associated with illegal immigrants, who sometimes commit additional crimes once they are living within the United States.

One estimate of the total Federal, state, and local cost of illegal immigrants to America is about $135 Billion. Even if you subtract the estimated taxes paid by illegal immigrants of $19 Billion, the net cost to American taxpayers is still a whopping $116 Billion, or roughly almost $2,800 per illegal alien.[127]

This issue also divides along more philosophical and cultural lines as well. Some Leftists believe in open borders and an open society. In fact, some simply do not believe in any borders for America at all. They think anyone should be free to come into America and anyone should be free to live here if they wish.

Many conservatives present a different point of view when it comes to open borders or even closed borders that are effectively porous, due to inadequate enforcement. They believe that illegal immigration is a matter of our civilizational survival. For them, if America allows in too many illegal immigrants (or for that matter, too many legal immigrants) who refuse to assimilate into American culture, it will result in the virtual collapse of American civilization, as we have experienced it for nearly two and a half centuries.

Of course, many conservatives are concerned that short of civilizational collapse, illegal immigration is nevertheless a serious and sobering national security issue. These conservatives believe that illegal immigration can result in terrorists slipping across our borders unnoticed and wreaking havoc in our cities on a level comparable to the attacks in Europe in recent years.

Also, conservatives think that illegal and unfettered immigration can lead to additional national security threats, including severe gang related violence imposed on some Americans by the cruel and brutal M13 gang.

Another more virulent and potentially widespread threat comes from the spread of possible diseases and epidemics, such as Yellow Fever, Dengue Fever, tuberculosis, and chikungunya, the so-called "virus of pain." All of these disease and epidemic threats have appeared in Central America in recent years and can be carried across our open border on the south by illegal immigrants that are not screened for health issues.[128]

What is Our Lottery System for Awarding Visas?

Clouding the issue of illegal immigration further are the appropriate concerns over existing laws. Questions come up about whether or not any immigration laws should be based on a lottery system that permits new immigrants into America with only a minimum level of education or work experience, and regardless of their desire to adapt to a new culture or political system.

Failure to assimilate into America, for example, is a clear recipe for a variety of significant cultural, political, and economic problems.

Incidentally, our current lottery system is called the Diversity Immigrant Visa Program (or DV Program). It is run by the State Department and permits up to 50,000 immigrants annually to receive immigrant visas from countries that have low immigration rates. Selection of immigrants is conducted by a random process from those who have specifically applied.[129] What criteria does the State Department use to screen potential immigrants?

There are a number of rules for applying for a Diversity Immigrant Visa, but the principal requirements for applicants are that they are from a country with a low immigration rate, plus they must have either a high school education or two years of work experience.[130]

Of course, conservatives think it makes more sense to give immigrant visas to those who bring to America a much needed skill such as a doctor, an engineer, or a software developer. Also, conservatives stress the importance of the desire to fit-in and assimilate into American culture.

If a potential new legal immigrant is uncomfortable with America's political system consisting of a Constitutional republic and widespread freedom, will they be an overall plus to America? Certainly, it doesn't make sense to allow new immigrants into America, who fundamentally disagree with our political system and its major long term policies. Put more directly, anti-American terrorists especially and others, who reject America's cultural and political system, need to be screened out of the legal immigration system.

The current lottery system for awarding visas seems to have few advantages and a number of significant drawbacks.

What is Chain Migration?
Another related issue is chain migration. **Chain migration** is simply the ability of legal immigrants once in America to sponsor their relatives to become legal immigrants as well. Let's look at it

in more detail.

When a person is given permission to come to the United States, the person's entire nuclear family can be admitted as well. The nuclear family is the original immigrant, their spouse, and their minor children.[131] That is simple immigration.

Chain migration begins when the original immigrants and their spouse become naturalized citizens. At that point, they can petition for their parents to come to America, along with their adult children, and their spouses and their children. In addition, the original immigrant and their spouse can also petition for their adult brothers and sisters to come to America as well.[132]

It's easy to see how the number of legal immigrants can expand greatly through chain migration.

In a perhaps unanticipated way, chain migration has led to a certain level of illegal immigration. The reason is that some families, while waiting for legal immigration through chain migration, grow tired of the process. They anticipate eventual legal immigration, but annual immigration caps and per-country limits delay their ultimate green cards. So, they simply come to America and stay illegally, thinking they will become legal immigrants sometime in the future.[133]

As with the lottery system, chain migration is based on the family chain relationship, not a certain level of skills, education, or desire to assimilate into American culture.

The current chain migration system for awarding visas seems to have few advantages and a number of drawbacks similar to the lottery system.

DACA Participants vs. DREAMers
In the immigration debate, two terms come up frequently and they are sometimes used interchangeably and this can be a source of confusion in the debate. Let's look at these two terms.

DACA stands for Deferred Action for Childhood Arrivals. It is an immigration policy and program established by the Obama administration in 2012 that allowed some younger illegal immigrants to obtain renewable two year work visas and avoid deportation. It ultimately applied to about 700,000 illegal immigrants.[134] When it was initiated, Republicans complained that it was not legal for President Obama to modify existing immigration law or to make new immigration law.

DACA was rescinded by President Trump in September 2017 with a six month phase-out period. During the phase-out, no new DACA applications would be accepted and granted. President Trump essentially bounced the question of DACA participants back to Congress. Since DACA was never created by Congressional legislative action, he was simply enforcing existing immigration law as it was originally written.

From President Trump's perspective at the time, if Congress felt young illegal immigrants should get work permits, then they needed to enact new legislation. President Trump seemed amenable to signing such a bill, if it were passed by Congress.

The term DREAMers seems to have originated in 2001 with Senate bill 1291 that year. The bill was called the Development, Relief, and Education for Alien Minors (DREAM) Act. It was intended to help illegal immigrants, who came to the U. S. as children, to develop a path to permanent legal status. It required certain criteria be met, such as attendance or completion of higher education, and not have violated other immigration laws.[135]

Since that time probably more than 20 bills (DREAM bills or bills that incorporate similar features) have been proposed in Congress, but none of them have ever made it into law. Illegal immigrants that might become participants in any potential DREAM program have come to be known as DREAMers.[136]

DACA was an Obama administration attempt to create new immigration legislation when no DREAM act could pass Congress. Republicans balked at the program as being outside current immigration laws. The Obama administration positioned the program in a category they called prosecutorial discretion. They were choosing not to prosecute this group of illegal immigrants.

The confusion between DACA participants and DREAMers arises because the two groups are not the same. While there are about 700,000 DACA participants, the estimate of likely DREAMers who fit the legislative requirements are about 3 million or more illegal immigrants.[137]

Some conservatives believe that the Left chooses to confuse DACA participants and DREAMers because Americans are more sympathetic to DACA participants. Then, if any new DACA immigration law passes that includes the broader DREAMers criteria embedded in the legislation, then millions of additional illegal immigrants will be included. Some conservatives believe the Left wants them to gain amnesty and citizenship, helping to fill the voter rolls with new voters who will support Leftist political candidates.

The bottom line is that even though many people in the illegal immigration debate use the terms DACA participants and DREAMers interchangeably, they are not synonyms. Part of the political issue on DACA is whether or not to include the larger illegal immigration group called DREAMers in any new legislation.

In addition to all the issues surrounding legal and illegal immigration, the enforcement of immigration laws, and even the creation of potential new immigration laws, a prominent and related political issue during the 2016 presidential election was building a secure fence to secure our borders.

Will We Protect Our Borders by Building a Secure Fence?

Building a secure fence to protect our borders was a signature issue of Trump's presidential campaign. Whether it is paid for by Mexico directly or paid for by Congress with the money being recouped through various programs is yet to be determined. But, building a secure fence is clearly an item high on President Trump's agenda.

Incidentally, there is discussion over precisely what constitutes a secure fence. Is it a continuous 2,000 mile long physical fence? Is it a physical fence in key locations and a technologically enforced fence in other areas? Is it protected by a significantly increased force of border agents?

President Trump's request for border security in early 2018 includes:

- About $18 Billion for 700 miles of new and replacement border barriers, bringing the total U. S. – Mexico fence to about 1,000 miles in length (out of the 2,000 mile border between the two countries),
- About $9 Billion for additional Border Security agents and other personnel,
- About $6 Billion for towers, surveillance equipment, unmanned aerial vehicles, and additional technology, and
- About $1 Billion for road construction and maintenance.[138]

The expenditures are spread over a number of years. Instead of calling it simply a "wall" as was done during the presidential campaign, it is sometimes called a "wall system."[139]

Not surprisingly, the Left vociferously oppose the wall or the wall system and its attendant costs, while conservatives believe it is absolutely needed to protect America from terrorists, drug dealers, gangs, and others. Conservatives also support building a secure fence because they think it is needed to rein in illegal immigration and its many economic problems.

President Trump has tied approval of funding for the wall system as well as elimination of the lottery system for approving visas and the elimination of chain migration, all to approval of DACA legislation. It is a strong negotiating stance.

The final component of the multi-faceted immigration issue is sanctuary cities.

Will We Continue to Allow Sanctuary Cities to Ignore the Rule of Law?

Sanctuary cities, or actually more broadly, sanctuary jurisdictions (there can be sanctuary states and sanctuary counties as well) are places in the U. S. where policies or laws are in place to limit local law enforcement agencies from working or cooperating with Federal immigration officials.

Sanctuary cities and sanctuary states are usually places that vote for progressive and socialist Democrats. Blue states and blue coastal cities are often sanctuary jurisdictions.

Sanctuary states include California, Oregon, Connecticut, Rhode Island, and Vermont.[140] Not unexpectedly, sanctuary cities include: Los Angeles, San Francisco, Berkeley, Chicago, Baltimore, Washington, and Boston.[141]

Generally, the limitations imposed by sanctuary jurisdictions on their law enforcement officers include not asking someone stopped by police about the person's immigration status and not notifying the Immigration and Customs Enforcement (ICE) agency when illegal immigrants are released from jail.

Conservatives think that sanctuary jurisdictions are flaunting the spirit as well as the letter of the immigration laws in question by selectively choosing to ignore Federal law. Conservatives believe that the primarily reason for their permissive stand on immigration laws is to effectively increase the number of illegal immigrants living in the U. S. Those additional immigrants might eventually become naturalized citizens and probably future supporters of Leftwing politics and politicians.

Conservatives also believe that blue states and blue cities are risking the safety of their citizens just to boost their chances of gaining future left-leaning voters. To conservatives, it makes no sense to protect illegal immigrant felons, even some with multiple felony convictions, from deportation from America.

How will America deal with the complexities of immigration, illegal immigration, and the distinctly different viewpoints surrounding these political issues in the next few years?

Prediction #5 – The Future of American Immigration and Related Issues

During the new Conservative Era that America has entered as a result of the historic and critical presidential election of 2016, I predict American immigration law and its enforcement will dramatically change over the next few years.

First, I predict the Trump administration will move aggressively to enforce existing immigration laws that have largely been glossed over or ignored in recent years under the previous administration. We will follow the law instead of thwarting the law. Taking this simple step will noticeably resolve much of the issue and will appreciably limit illegal immigration.

Conservatives believe in the Rule of Law and equal justice under the law. Conservatives believe that laws are not made to be selectively enforced. Elite politicians can't skirt the law through clever legal maneuvers, any more than foreign nationals can subvert the law by climbing over border barriers in America's southwest.

Conservatives believe every citizen needs to follow the law in America. During this new Conservative Era, we can expect immigration laws in particular will get enforced vigorously.

To illustrate, many immigrants have entered America legally, but then violated their visas. Tighter monitoring and enforcement of visas is a straight forward step to make immigration law more effective.

Use of workplace monitoring and use of the e-verify system will be substantially enhanced across America to stem the tide of illegal immigrants obtaining and keeping jobs while living here in violation of our laws. Similarly, restricting the ability of illegal immigrants to cash checks in the United States, will markedly cut down on illegal immigration that is based on the economic incentives of living in America.

Expect new legislation as well to eliminate both the lottery system for awarding visas and chain migration for allowing many more legal immigrants. Expect the new immigration legislation to allow in immigrants using a merit-based visa system in place of the lottery system and chain migration programs.

Plus, we can also expect a legislative compromise on the DACA program that will allow most DACA participants to stay and work in the United States, while providing most of the funds sought by the president for a secure fence. Although elements of previous DREAM legislation will be considered, it is highly unlikely that such a DREAM proposal will ever be enacted into law.

President Trump will likely endorse and sign the new comprehensive immigration law that will end the lottery system for awarding visas, will end the chain migration program, will require the e-verify system, and will substantially fund border security with a secure wall system. It will also allow DACA participants to apply for and receive work visas. Increased enforcement of current and new immigration laws will be implemented by the Trump administration.

Eventually, the Trump administration will win the lawsuits preventing it from withholding funds from sanctuary cities that continue to harbor illegal immigrants that are felons. Expect the lawsuits to take time to work their way through the court system.

Let's turn our attention now to the upcoming elections.

Part IV

What Will Happen in the Upcoming Elections and in the Future?

Chapter 11

What Will Happen in the Upcoming Elections and in American Politics?

After the Roy Moore loss in the Alabama Senate race in December 2017, Democrats began using the term "blue wave" more often to refer to the potential Democratic Party sweep of the Congressional elections in 2018. One article even went so far as to say the loss had "ominous implications for the Republican Party in 2018."[142]

Those who studied the Roy Moore loss recognize that he did not campaign enough on the bread-and-butter issues that brought victory to presidential candidate Trump and to other conservative political candidates. As with many other campaigns in the past, conservative voters will frequently sit out an election that is not issue-focused on the specific areas of concern they consider vital. These voters think they don't have a candidate in the race that matters, so to them there is no point to voting.

The Roy Moore loss, along with Republican losses in the gubernatorial races in New Jersey and Virginia, don't signal a blue wave during the upcoming Congressional elections. These losses are outliers. They don't support the long-range and short-range trends that are driving American politics during the new Conservative Era.

Just as I do not see a blue wave coming, I don't see a red wave coming either. What does this mean for America? Plus, what is coming in the upcoming Congressional elections instead?

Will there be a Blue Wave, Red Wave, or Conservative Wave?

If America were to see a blue wave Congressional election, both the House and Senate would be captured by the Democratic Party and they would control the House and Senate for at least two years. Similarly, with a red wave Congressional election, we would expect Republicans to maintain control of the House and Senate for at least two more years.

But, when we refer to a red wave Congressional election, we really mean primarily an Establishment Republican sweep of both the House and Senate. Establishment Republicans would in essence control both legislative bodies. There is a third alternative.

We might see a conservative wave Congressional election. In this scenario, the Republican Party would maintain control of the House and Senate, but importantly, the makeup of the Republican caucuses in the House and Senate would be more conservative. In effect, it would be a conservative red wave.

A conservative wave election would follow through on the same long-range and short-range trends that propelled presidential candidate Trump into the White House. It would be one step closer to the ultimate split of the Republican Party into two new parties, the Conservative Party and the Republican Progressive Party.

How will the conservative wave take place? Many Establishment Republicans will see the strong support for conservative principles and policies among their constituents and choose to not seek reelection. They might retire outright or simply they might decide to end their political career and return to the private sector.

Other Establishment Republicans might decide to fight the conservative wave and would seek reelection. Many will then face stiff opposition from conservative primary challengers, who are swimming with the conservative wave. Some Establishment Republicans will lose out to their conservative primary opponents. Later in November, conservative primary challengers will have an edge in their general election bids against progressive socialists running on the Democratic Party side.

Besides impacting the Republican Party, a conservative wave election would also significantly influence the Democratic Party. Expect that Democratic Party officeholders will continue to lose elections as their political ideology, programs, and policies are rejected by the American voter.

In particular, Democrats that staked out strong positions against President Trump in his efforts to carry out the mandate of the 2016 presidential election and fulfill his agenda will be at risk of losing their seats in office. Democrats, who spent considerable time and effort in the "resistance" movement against President Trump since his inauguration, will be especially vulnerable during the Congressional elections.

Some Democratic Party incumbents might even face more conservative Democratic Party primary challengers.

The net effect of a conservative wave would be continued Republican Congressional control and overall a more conservative House and Senate.

Will the Republican Party Continue to Control the House?

Let's first start by looking at where the House stands going into the upcoming Congressional elections. How is it divided politically?

The Republican Party controls the House by about 20 seats more than the 218 minimum number of seats required to control the House of Representatives. Of course, many of these seats are considered **"safe seats"** because they are usually carried by the incumbent's party and they will probably stay in that party's control after the election.

Approximately 20 seats are likely **"toss-up seats."** Either party might win any of these toss-up seats in the Congressional elections. Sometimes a toss-up seat gains that status when an incumbent decides to retire or not seek reelection and the Congressional District in question is reasonably competitive without an incumbent in place.

Another 35 seats I call **"contentious seats."** Contentious seats are seats whose Congressional districts split their votes by party in the previous presidential election and Congressional election. For example, in Minnesota's Congressional District 8 (CD-8) in 2016, Democratic incumbent Rick Nolan won over Republican challenger Stewart Mills with these results:

- Rick Nolan (D) – 50.2%
- Stewart Mills (R) – 49.6%[143]

But, in 2016, Trump carried Minnesota CD-8 over Clinton:

- Donald Trump (R) – 54.2%
- Hillary Clinton (D) – 38.6% [144]

Notice how Republican presidential candidate Donald Trump carried Minnesota's CD-8 with about 54% of the votes, while Republican Congressional District candidate Stewart Mills lost the CD-8 race with approximately 49% of the voters in the district. This is a contentious seat because the reasons for the split between presidential and Congressional candidates seem to be in conflict.

I believe the Republican Party will lose a few more toss-up and contentious seats than the Democratic Party, but will still be in control of the House with about 232 seats to the Democrats 203 seats.

Importantly, I think the ideological makeup of the new House will be decidedly more conservative.

Let's look at the Senate next.

Will the Republican Party Continue to Control the Senate?

Going into the upcoming Congressional elections, the Republicans control the Senate 51 – 49 seats with Vice President Pence available for a tie-breaker Republican vote should the Senate deadlock at 50 – 50 for a particular vote. Up for reelection are 23 Democratic Party Senate seats, 2 Independents that caucus with the Democratic Party, and eight Republican seats.

Three Republican incumbent Senators have chosen not to run for reelection thus far. They are: Sen. Jeff Flake of Arizona, Sen. Bob Corker of Tennessee, and Sen. Orrin Hatch of Utah.

Of the 34 Senate seats, about five Senate seats are probably considered toss-up seats. Eleven seats are contentious seats. The Democratic Party is at risk of losing ten of the 11 contentious seats. Some of the five toss-up seats are also contentious seats.

I believe the American voters are not satisfied with the pace and progress of the Senate relative to the Trump mandate and agenda. But, I think American voters will not opt for a blue wave election because they are dissatisfied with the Democratic Party even more than they are dissatisfied with the Republican Party establishment.

I think the Republican Party will pick up a minimum of six Senate seats, but more likely, about nine Senate seats in the upcoming Congressional elections. Once again, I think the Senate will move several steps closer to being a conservative legislative body.

Remember, too, that the Founding Fathers designed the Senate within the Constitution to be a political institution that would change slowly. They did so with the clear intent to protect our nation from change that was too rapid and ill-considered. Today, the Senate is moving in the direction of the new Conservative Era in a measured and careful manner, albeit too slow for many conservatives.

Will the New Senate be Filibuster-Proof?
With nine additional Senate seats added to the existing 51 seats, Republicans will have 60 Senate seats and a filibuster-proof Senate. With so many new members, Senate leadership will probably change hands as well.

In the new Senate, conservative legislation will have a much easier time of getting passed. The backlog of House bills that have been held up by the Senate will finally begin to get tackled by the

Senate.

Will there be a Conservative Super-Majority on the Supreme Court?

Expect the new and more conservative Senate to easily confirm the three new Constitutional conservative justices to the Supreme Court that President Trump will likely get to appoint before the end of his first term. I anticipate Justices Ruth Bader Ginsburg, Anthony Kennedy, and Stephen Breyer will all retire during Trump's administration.

Their replacement appointments will glide through the Senate with minimal committee hearings and other red tape, although the Left will no likely continue to complain vehemently about the conservative bent of the new Supreme Court to no avail.

America will have a conservative super-majority on the Supreme Court that will last until about the year 2050 and beyond, based on the average age of Supreme Court appointments and retirements. This super-majority will have a profoundly positive impact on America in the future.

It will also restore the balance of judicial restraint and judicial activism to more originalist thinking within the judicial system. Judges will relinquish their assumed legislative roles in favor of the traditional role of interpreting the laws and judging outcomes based on the Constitution and those laws.

Conservative appointments to Federal District Courts and Circuit Courts of Appeal will continue at a healthy and record pace compared with any recent president's appointment record.

Will the New Congress be More Conservative?

Overall, will the new Congress, House and Senate, produce more conservative legislation? Count on it.

The long-range trends and short-range trends that I have studied largely point in the direction of the new Conservative Era that I predicted and discussed in *Great News for America*.[145]

As I have written, America is seeking morality and freedom, peace and prosperity. Conservative principles are the proven guidelines to achieve those objectives. Progressive socialism, democratic socialism, socialism, Marxism, communism, and anarchism only guarantee that a nation will sink into moral and economic bankruptcy. They do little or nothing to advance a nation's spiritual and material well-being.

The new, more conservative Congress will move the voter's agenda, the conservative agenda, the Trump agenda, forward in leaps and bounds. But, I think the full extent of what the voters seek will only be realized when the Republican Party splits into two separate and distinct parties, the Conservative Party and the Republican Progressive Party.

In reality, the American voters are pushing the Republican Party into becoming a Conservative Party. But, many in the old Establishment Republican Party don't want to follow the direction of the voters. It's easier for them to pursue the old ways, the old alliances, the old donors, the old lobbyists, the old programs, the old policies, and the old power they have had and continue to hold onto so tightly.

As the new Conservative Era rolls out throughout America, the political parties will change and will eventually catch up with the American people.

Congress will continue to become more conservative as they fully understand the views of the American voter and incorporate it into their legislation.

But, what about millennials and their impact on the new conservative Congress? What about their affinity and their desire for socialism and communism? Will they derail the new Conservative Era?

Will Millennials Derail the New Conservative Era?

With our K-12 primary and secondary education system, along with our colleges and universities, mostly focused on political indoctrination rather than education and learning, it is no wonder why so many millennials seem ignorant about the benefits of freedom, free markets, free enterprise, and capitalism. It's also no surprise that in various surveys of millennials they often choose socialism and communism over capitalism.

Recall, for example, the article cited earlier that 58% of American millennials would prefer to live under socialism, communism, or fascism. Only 42% favored capitalism.[146]

Not surprisingly, many conservatives are troubled by these studies and wonder whether millennials will derail the new Conservative Era.

As we will see in the last chapter, the political viewpoints of millennials are in early transition. With the renaissance of reason starting to take place, we will see millennials adopt more conservative thinking and viewpoints. Millennials will support, and in many cases, will be active participants in the new Conservative Era.

Returning to the new, more conservative Congress, will the leadership remain the same or will it change hands?

Will the New Congress Continue with the Same Leadership Team?

As part of the growing Conservative Era, expect that both the House and Senate will change its respective leadership teams. This is a natural consequence of a decidedly more conservative Congress. New leaders in both the House and Senate will be able to move the new conservative agenda ahead more quickly and easily.

Also, expect the new leadership teams to come from the ranks of the conservative members of the Republican Party, until a

Conservative Party ultimately emerges on the American political scene. Then, the House and Senate will be led by the Conservative Party's leaders.

Will the New Congress Support the Trump Agenda?

Yes, the new, more conservative Congress will support President Trump and his agenda for the nation.

While there might be some disagreements between the president and Congress over timing, budget, and the implementation of specific agenda items, they will be relatively minor compared to the vehement and vitriolic opposition of the Left immediately following President Trump's election in 2016 and his first year in office in 2017.

Prediction #6 – A Conservative Wave

With regard to the upcoming Congressional elections, I predict a conservative wave election with the Republican Party maintaining control of the House and Senate. Importantly, I predict the composition of the House and Senate will both be more conservative, with quite a few Establishment Republicans and Establishment Democrats losing their current seats and being replaced with more conservative members.

I think the conservative wave election will also usher in new, more conservative House and Senate leadership.

I predict the new Congress with substantially support President Trump and the Trump agenda for the nation. I expect the new Congress will swing into action and quickly begin to pass new conservative legislation.

I expect the Senate to easily confirm President Trump's likely three new conservative originalist appointees to the Supreme Court. During President Trump's first term in office, I predict America will have a conservative super-majority on the Supreme Court.

Prediction #7 – The Next Presidential Election

Looking forward to the 2020 presidential election, my early prediction is that President Trump will be reelected fairly easily with a greater Electoral College victory than in 2016. Currently, I predict he will win the Electoral College with over 350 Electoral Votes and a popular vote victory margin exceeding 3% of the actual vote total.

The reasons for these conclusions include many trends, factors, and realities. Consider these vital points. First, all the major long-range trends that propelled presidential candidate Trump into office remain intact. Second, all the significant short-range trends that favored Trump's victory are still in place.

In addition, many dynamic election factors are setting up in President Trump's corner. These include:

- Voter Intensity
- Voter Registration Dynamics
- Voter Enthusiasm
- Voter Optimism
- Voter Peace and National Security Perception
- Voter Prosperity and Economic Security Perception

Plus, the economy has taken off for the first time in about a decade. GDP growth is about 3.2% in the third quarter of 2017 with some near-term forecasts of 4% and higher. That means Americans will be feeling economically optimistic and strong going into the 2020 presidential election with more money in their checking accounts and in the 401Ks. Without a doubt, a good economy helps the incumbent president.

On the vital jobs front, the unemployment rate for December 2017, released in January 2018, is 4.1% on an overall downward trend since the election of President Trump.[147] That's a plus as well for President Trump's reelection.

In foreign policy, President Trump took decisive action to booster America's security and leadership in the world.

President Trump was decisive in dealing with Syria's use of chemical weapon against its own people. Helpless men, women, and children were brutally choked to death. The president ordered a military attack on Shayrat air base near Homs. Subsequently, 59 Tomahawk Land Attack Missiles, launched from the destroyers USS Porter and USS Ross in the eastern Mediterranean, sent a clear signal to Syria that America would not tolerate the use of chemical weapons against innocent citizens.[148]

President Trump also gave U. S. military commanders and troops on the ground full authority to defeat ISIS and their hateful ideology. ISIS strongholds in both Raqqah (former ISIS capital) and Mosul have fallen. The end of the ISIS Caliphate scourge seems near, further protecting Americans at home, and other freedom-loving people around the world.[149]

Recall how ISIS threatened to have their soldiers attack America and Americans in our homeland. For example, Fox News reported that a self-described jihadist said that ISIS has 71 trained soldiers in the United States in 15 States ready to carry out operations against America. This unsettling threat went so far as to name five of the 15 States that were said to have ISIS soldiers: Virginia, Maryland, Illinois, California, and Michigan.[150]

President Trump moved decisively to remove and eliminate the threat of ISIS to America.

Another threat, the threat of North Korea, with its potential for nuclear-tipped ICBMs, potentially arrayed against America's homeland and our military forces on Guam, appears to be diminished now as well.

No doubt this is due to President Trump's tough words and his strong show of military force with three aircraft carrier strike groups off the North Korean peninsula. The three aircraft carrier task groups are led by the USS Ronald Reagan, the USS Nimitz, and the USS Theodore Roosevelt, all Nimitz-class aircraft carriers.[151]

All of these trends, factors, and realities indicate that President

Trump will be reelected president in 2020 with a greater percentage of popular votes and a greater Electoral College margin than in 2016.

Let's move on and discuss why there is more great news for America in our future.

Chapter 12

How and Why the Good Guys Win in the End!

America has been engaged in a great battle for its very existence. Our freedom, free markets, and free enterprise have been in jeopardy for a long time. The institutions upon which our freedoms are built – namely, the Church, the Constitution, and the Family – have been under relentless assault by the Left.

Why have the Church, the Constitution, and the Family been under attack? It's simple. These three institutions are necessary to have freedom in our lives. Without these three institutions, we can't sustain freedom and we can't sustain the America that our Founding Fathers created, which I believe was inspired by God.

What about the Separation of Church and State?

Note that I want to make a quick point before continuing on. If a few readers are uncomfortable with me bringing up God in a book about politics, I do not think freedom can exist in the absence of God in our lives. That might surprise some.

From my research and study of both politics and freedom, I have come to the conclusion that in order to have freedom, we must have morality in our government and in our lives. Obviously, men and women are not angels. We all need to strive for morality in our lives. Our society is best when it's based on morality and the Rule of Law. Without morality and the Rule of Law, a nation deteriorates into either totalitarianism or anarchism or both.

Today, many people feel that there must be a strict "wall of separation" between Church and state. They think that government and state can't co-exist in any meaningful way. You have heard these types of stories or similar stories before, for years:

- You can't have the Ten Commandments posted in a Kentucky Courthouse.[152]
- You can't have a 29-foot Cross on top of the Mt. Soledad Veterans Memorial in San Diego because the land is owned by the U. S. Department of Defense.[153]

In my view, this so-called "wall of separation" between Church and state is based on a faulty reading of the First Amendment to the Constitution that clearly states: "Congress shall make no law respecting an establishment of religion; or prohibiting the free exercise thereof ..." This means, of course, that the government can't establish a religion for the nation. Congress can't decide we shall become a Catholic country and owe our allegiance to the Pope. Or, Congress can't make a law that our national religion is Judaism and only people of the Jewish faith can be hired by the Federal government for job openings.

The First Amendment also means the government can't prohibit anyone from freely exercising their chosen religion. Everyone should be free to attend their own Church, Synagogue, Mosque, or other religious place of worship and prayer. Everyone should be free to pray, or read the Bible, or wear religious jewelry, or wear a t-shirt with a religious message printed on it.

To my agnostic and atheistic friends and readers, I understand you might hold a different perspective than mine. That's the great benefit of freedom, we can hold different opinions. I do choose to mention God when thinking about politics and freedom because I believe that both our freedom and our political form of government are uniquely derived from, and built upon, our Judeo-Christian heritage.[154]

Let's return now to the great battle for government control versus individual freedom in America that has been raging for decades.

Indeed, forces favoring government control of our lives – our spiritual, moral, cultural, political, and economic lives – have been arrayed against the proponents of religious freedom, political freedom, and economic freedom in America.

I strongly believe that the good guys will win this battle in the end. But, who are the good guys?

The American People are the Good Guys

The American people are the good guys in American History. The American people sought morality, freedom, peace, and prosperity throughout our history. They also sought these same rock-solid principles during the 2016 historic and critical presidential election. They elected presidential candidate Trump to the shock of many in the media, in the Democratic Party, and on the Left.

The American people want and expect morality in government. They will not tolerate corruption in their government. They will not tolerate politicians for long that make campaign promises, but never deliver on those promises.

It's true that the American people are patient and will give politicians and political parties time in office to perform. But, eventually, they will tire of waiting and they will vote politicians out of office.

The American people are also tolerant of political parties. They will give political parties more time to be responsive than they give some officeholders. Yet, the American people will also grow weary of political parties that are indifferent and unresponsive. If necessary, they will change the offending political parties in major political party realignments. Political party realignments are relatively rare, but they do occur when Americans become sufficiently angry, upset, and frustrated with their political parties.

The American people want and expect freedom in their lives. They believe it is the duty of the government to protect their freedom. The American people want the Constitution and the Rule of law followed.

They want the Federal government to defend the nation from foreign enemies, such as North Korea and Iran, as well as external threats such as terrorists, gangs, and drug lords that might slip across our borders.

They expect our military to be technologically, strategically, and tactically superior. They want their military to be the best in the world. They want their military personnel to be treated in the best possible way while on active duty, and to be taken care of in the best possible way as military veterans.

The American people want peace with other nations, and peace inside our nation. The American people support their police, firefighters, and other first responders, and expect them to be protected from crime while performing their important duties.

The American people want prosperity and expect the government to support our economy with appropriate pro-growth tax policies, spending policies, regulatory policies, and monetary policies. They want and expect the government at all levels to enhance and empower the economy, and certainly not get in the way of, or restrain, economic growth and prosperity.

The American people continue to seek the fundamental conservative principles of morality, freedom, peace, and prosperity today. The American people support political parties, and elect political candidates, that they deem to be worthy of the responsibilities of their respective political offices. They seek officeholders that will advance morality, freedom, peace, and prosperity.

In truth, the American people are the good guys. They have good objectives. They seek good fundamental conservative principles. The American people, the good guys, will win in the end!

How Will the Good Guys Win in the End?

The good guys will win in the end by voting in elections across the nation, from the school board, to the county courthouse, to the State house, to the Congress, and to the White House. Elections, both primaries and general elections, drive our government.

Elections determine officeholders directly in races large and small. They also decide political appointees indirectly for some government departments and agencies. They also control appointments to many judicial slots that include Supreme Court Justices, the Circuit Courts of Appeal judges, and the Federal District judges, as well as State and local judges.

Elections are responsible for staffing our government at the Federal, State, and local levels.

By electing certain politicians representing specific political parties, we also are likely endorsing particular political platforms, policies, programs, and often specific legislative proposals. Voting in elections is our means for controlling government and influencing our future.

Just as physical momentum is a significant force in the physical world (think about a car driving out-of-control off an icy road in the winter), political momentum is a powerful force in the world of politics. The good guys will tend to vote for their political party for years or decades on end, rarely deviating from their basic choices.

However, if the America people are dissatisfied with officeholders, politicians, and the political parties over issues related to morality, freedom, peace, and prosperity, the good guys develop a sense of moral outrage. When the moral outrage of the American people reaches a crescendo of disappointment, frustration, and anger with the government, the moral outrage triggers an electoral tipping point.

Such a tipping point results in a cascade of varying political changes, including, possible changes in actual officeholders, and potential changes in political party control of the White House, the Senate, the House of Representatives, Governor's seats, State Houses, State Senates, and a myriad of other State and local offices.

In addition, such an electoral tipping point can mean changes to political planks in party platforms, entire political platforms, political philosophies, political party leadership, political party realignments, and political institution realignments. An example of political institution realignment is the coming conservative super-majority in the Supreme Court.

The vital point here is that the good guys wield enormous control over government by voting. Throughout American History, whenever the American people became morally outraged with their government, they used elections to reform, restore, and reinvigorate their government.

As I discussed in my book, *Great News for America*,[155] the year 2016 would be an historic and critical presidential election and it would usher in a new American Constitutional Era, the Conservative Era. We can expect to see in the next few election cycles the rollout of the Conservative Era in American politics.

We will likely see the good guys win primarily by voting in elections across the nation.

Voting Integrity and Voter ID are Necessary for the Good Guys to Win

Voting may be the single most important duty of any citizen in America. But, voting is not sufficient to assure the smooth functioning of any free nation, including America. Why?

I believe that free men and free women will generally vote in their best interests. In America, the good guys will usually vote in historic and critical presidential elections because they believe that they are voting for some or all of the four fundamental principles of morality, freedom, peace, and prosperity. However, simply voting is no guarantee that the will of the American voters will be reflected in the actual election results.

A number of possible problems can arise with the voting process and these problems can taint the election results. These problems can even cause the wrong person to be declared the winner in an election. For example, if the voter registration process lacks common sense checks and balances that might occur due to the implementation of same-day voter registration or motor voter registration or other novel voting practices, voter fraud can take place relatively easily.

If safeguards are not in place (such as the use of local databases) and people are allowed to vote multiple times in a given jurisdiction that can cause problems for the voting process. Similarly, if statewide safeguards are not in place (such as the use of multiple state or local databases) and people are allowed to vote multiple times in different jurisdictions that cross multiple state or local boundaries, once again election results might be blatantly off from the true will of the actual legal voters.

Other problems can arise as well. If some illegal immigrants (who are clearly not legal citizens in America) are allowed to vote (by a politically-motivated wayward sanctuary state, county, or city) or if some illegal immigrants are allowed to vote simply by a lack of sufficient voter registration validation controls being in place, these situations can throw off election results.

Depending on the state, convicted felons might or might not be permitted by law to vote. The following restrictions listed are as of 2016. Some states like Maine and Vermont have no voting restrictions on felons. Some states like Montana and Michigan restrict felons who are inmates from voting, while other states like California and Colorado restrict felons, who are inmates or parolees.[156]

There are other states that are tougher still that restrict felons, who are inmates, parolees, or probationers from voting. Texas and Louisiana are examples of these states that further restrict felons.[157]

The most restrictive states for felons don't permit inmates, parolees, probationers, or even ex-cons from voting at all. Examples of these states include Nevada and Arizona.[158]

If any felons who are restricted by their respective states laws, violate these laws, and vote anyway, it is a form of voter fraud.

Whatever the cause of voter fraud, it must be curtailed to the extent possible, and preferably, it must be completely eliminated. Otherwise, the will of American voters can be dramatically altered.

One common sense solution is to require by law that all citizens use Voter ID to register to vote, and before actually voting, in an election. This makes a lot of sense when we consider the importance of voting and involving citizens in the governing of the nation. It also makes sense since citizens need ID for many other commonplace activities, such as going through security at an airport, purchasing alcohol in many places, and even obtaining a library card.

Yet, Leftists oppose Voter ID laws that require potential voters to produce identification before registering to vote and before voting. Leftists argue that Voter ID requirements pose an undue hardship on some voters and therefore, will suppress voter turnout. In truth, Voter ID does not suppress voting, it suppresses voter fraud.

The reality is that most nations around the world require Voter ID and apparently don't believe that Voter ID is a burden on their citizens. According to John Fund, "The vast majority of countries require voter ID — usually photo ID — to prevent fraud and duplicate votes at the polls."[158]

Why shouldn't America (that values morality and freedom so highly) also require Voter ID laws to assure voter integrity?

To illustrate how lack of voter integrity might impact the next presidential election, consider these six states with something in common in 2016:

- Florida – 29 Electoral Votes
- Michigan – 16 Electoral Votes
- Minnesota – 10 Electoral Votes
- New Hampshire – 4 Electoral Votes
- Pennsylvania – 20 Electoral Votes
- Wisconsin – 10 Electoral Votes

These six states were decided by about 1.5% or less of the popular votes in 2016. That represents a block of 89 Electoral Votes. Of the 89 Electoral Votes, Trump carried all but Minnesota and New Hampshire for a total of 75 Electoral Votes. Clinton received 14 Electoral Votes from this block.[160]

If voter fraud altered the popular vote by more than about 1.5% in any of these states, the Electoral College results might have changed. The number 1.5% is a reasonable amount to estimate for voter fraud under a significant voter fraud scenario.

Consider the State of New Hampshire. Newer data in New Hampshire indicates that on Election Day, November 8, 2016, greater than 6,500 people registered to vote in the state with out-of-state driver's licenses, relying on the state's same-day voter registration rules.[161]

Subsequently, it was learned that most of these voters never obtained a New Hampshire driver's license or registered a car in the state after the election. Some conservatives think this same-day voting was illegal voting by Democrat voters from Massachusetts that sought to influence the election outcome in New Hampshire for Clinton.[162]

In this case, there were 6,500 same-day voters in question[163] in a state carried by Clinton by only 2,732 votes.[164] It's possible if these votes were actually illegal votes, and had been prevented, and had never been counted, Trump would have carried the State of New Hampshire in the Electoral College instead of Clinton. However, New Hampshire's four Electoral Votes would not have altered the final outcome of Trump's Electoral College victory.

But, what this example points out is that voter fraud might impact some election results, some of the time. Of course, that's disconcerting for most voters, who genuinely seek honest elections. It's essential that America strive to assure voting integrity in all of its elections.

Voter ID is a necessity to guarantee voting integrity. At some point in the next few years, I anticipate all states and possibly Congress as well will pass reasonable, straightforward, and simple Voter ID laws to assure voting integrity across America.

Why Will the Good Guys Win in the End?

The good guys will win in the end because their objectives – the conservative principles of morality, freedom, peace, and prosperity – resonate in the hearts, souls, and minds of Americans in particular, and in men and women in general.

Simply put. The fundamental conservative principles of morality, freedom, peace, and prosperity are a winning game plan. They are a winning formula for a nation.

These principles are time-tested. When America follows these principles, America thrives. When America deviates from these principles, there is stress and distress. But, these periods of trial are replaced fairly quickly with times of moral and material improvement and progress.

The good guys will win in the end because they have good goals that resonate in their hearts, souls, and minds. Their goals fundamentally align with the human spirit.

These goals are also closely related to the idea of American Exceptionalism.

American Exceptionalism Will Win in the End

Indeed, freedom goes hand-in-hand with American Exceptionalism. Let's see why.

Freedom has been thought about, written about, talked about, and dreamed about over the centuries. It has been fought for and fought against repeatedly. It is of great significance and importance to men, women, and their lives. What precisely is freedom and how is it related to American Exceptionalism?

Freedom is the power to act (or not to act) within the framework of morality and one's own reason and free will. If you want to learn more about freedom, please read my book *Renewing America and*

Its Heritage of Freedom. [165]

American Exceptionalism is the idea that America was founded by the thirteen original states on the truth that freedom was a God given right of all men. In addition, American Exceptionalism stemmed from the further belief that the people could delegate a limited degree of freedom, for a limited time, to a government, for the purpose of the common good.

This is a key point. American Exceptionalism stood in stark contrast to other nations whose governments delegated limited freedoms to the people. Rather than limited freedom and limited power going from the government to the people, with American Exceptionalism, limited freedom and limited power went from the people to the government. This was, and still is, an exceptional approach to government.

Like the fundamental conservative principles of morality, freedom, peace, and prosperity, American Exceptionalism resonates in the hearts, souls, and minds of the American people. It is part of our religious, political, and economic heritage.

As a result, American Exceptionalism will win in the end.

Prediction #8 – The Dawning of a New Conservative Enlightenment

Voting in elections is the primary driver in moving America forward into the new Conservative Era.

But, in addition, I predict the dawning of a new Conservative Enlightenment that will further extend, strengthen, enhance, and then maintain our new Conservative Era for decades to come.

I predict the new Conservative Enlightenment will include 4 R's in America's future. These 4 R's are major, significant, religious and cultural trends. They will play an important role in developing and promoting America's religious freedom, political freedom, and economic freedom. They will also positively impact life in America on many different levels and in many different ways.

The 4 R's I predict are summarized here and explained in the sections that follow:

- The Return to Faith in God
- The Renaissance of Reason
- The Restoration of Education
- The Rebirth of Morality, Freedom, Peace, and Prosperity

Let's start with the return to faith in God.

The Return to Faith in God

Faith in God is necessary to build an effective political system of democracy. You can read about my reasons why this statement is true in one of my earlier books, if you are curious.[166]

Once such a political system is built and is functional, the political system does not require all of its citizens to have faith in God. Yet, all of its citizens, believers and non-believers, do benefit from the ensuing morality, freedom, peace, and prosperity.

I forecast a strong resurgence in faith in God in America. Part of this resurgence is a component of long-range trends that I have seen in my research and part is a component of some related short-range trends.

In addition to these reasons for a return to faith in God, I also forecast a spiritual human need that men and women will fulfill from having faith in God. Prior to the Conservative Era, many on the Left and many followers of the Left's ideology attempted to meet that spiritual human need through progressive socialism and its secular lifestyle. Of course, a secular ideology is inadequate to meet spiritual human needs.

With the religious, political, and economic failures of the Left's ideology, as well as the rejection of that ideology and lifestyle, I forecast the return to faith in God. As a result, expect Church and Synagogue attendance to increase in the future and expect negative cultural markers such as divorce rates to gradually decline over time.

The return to faith in God is closely related to the new Conservative Era and to the strengthening of America's religious freedom, political freedom, and economic freedom.

The Renaissance of Reason

The second of the 4 R's I forecast is the renaissance of reason. What do I mean by this trend?

The renaissance of reason is America's use of reason in everyday analysis and life. For years, America has been plagued by junk science with questionable studies and fake conclusions generated more to support politically correct positions, policies, and narratives, rather than to advance our civilization and society.

It's not my purpose here to delineate and catalog all the junk science we have witnessed in the last twenty years in America and around the world. Many books and comprehensive journal articles have been written to do just that. I have even written about a few of them over the years.

In this book, I want to forecast, as part of the new Conservative Era, that a considerable body of junk science and fake reports with dubious results will be exposed and debunked for what they truly represent – distorted science done for political purposes.

The renaissance of reason will start in America and will span the world with a renewed understanding of reason, logic, and scientific method, as well as a return to properly designed statistical experiments and verifiable experimental results. True scientists, physical and social scientists, who seek the truth and knowledge, will relish the renaissance of reason.

Expect many benefits to accrue from the renaissance of reason including the more effective use of research dollars, both in government sponsored R&D and in the private sector. Also, expect substantially improved innovation and productivity across nearly all industries and disciplines.

The Restoration of Education

Closely aligned to the renaissance of reason is the true restoration of education in America. It's the third R of the 4 R's and it is powerful in its long-range impact on America.

The deterioration of America's K-12 school system and America's colleges and universities is palpable, problematic, and reversible. Clearly, for anyone looking at America's educational system honestly, American education has been largely eliminated and replaced with decidedly obvious Leftist political indoctrination.

As part of the widespread indoctrination, free speech is curtailed, limited, threatened, and all but completely gone on American college campuses. In some places, free speech is limited to only a small space on campus, possibly for only a short time period each day. Isn't that ridiculous for an institution created for the purpose of educating people?

The Left has eliminated free speech and has indoctrinated students to promote the ISMs of Failure that they admire, support, and promote. Recall from the Preface in this book that the ISMs of Failure are progressive socialism, democratic socialism, socialism, Marxism, communism, and anarchism.

It's time in America to have free speech for all students in all schools, K-12, and on all college and university campuses. America is not a third world dictatorship. Our children and young adults need to be free once more to voice their opinions, express their thoughts, and be free to ask questions. We have a First Amendment. Let's start using it.

I forecast not only more free speech in American education, but and this is profound, the restoration of education. At the same time, I forecast the elimination of indoctrination in K-12 schools and in America's colleges and universities.

It's about to happen. The tipping point is close. It's all part of the new Conservative Era that values our freedom and our free speech. Yet, this forecast will take years to play out across America. There is a lot of work to be accomplished.

Indeed, the restoration of education will take time as new curricula are developed and K-12 teachers are updated on the principles of education and the avoidance of indoctrination of children in their classrooms. School boards will need to provide leadership and guidance. Parents will need to provide further oversight of school boards, principals, and teachers.

In higher education, college and university instructors and professors will need to be guided by their alumni, boards of trustees, administrators, and peers on the nature of education and the true objectives of education. They will once again have to seek education of students over the promotion of any personal ideologies that they might cling onto from their past.

Over time, during the new Conservative Era, I forecast the restoration of education will take place.

The Rebirth of Morality, Freedom, Peace, and Prosperity

Finally, I forecast the fourth R in the 4 R's that make up the new Conservative Enlightenment found in our growing Conservative Era. The fourth R is the rebirth of morality, freedom, peace, and prosperity.

The fourth R also refers to the results of having morality, freedom, peace, and prosperity in America. It's the blossoming of benefits associated with an increase in these four conservative principles.

More morality means less corruption in government. It also means the Constitution is followed more closely and the freedoms guaranteed by the Constitution are protected better by the government. More people also live within the Rule of Law. Violence and crime diminish in magnitude and scope as more and more citizens obey the law. Law officers are treated with respect. Property rights are protected and contracts are lived up to.

More freedom means all of the 25 essential components of our religious freedom, political freedom, and economic freedom are available to Americans.[167]

Examples that we can cite are abundant, but we list just a few for simplicity and brevity. To illustrate, free speech in our colleges and universities mentioned earlier is one essential component of freedom in a free nation. Another example is the freedom of conscience and action (part of religious freedom) in which a high school girl is allowed to express her Christian belief by wearing a Cross necklace to school.

Or, a third example of the essential components of freedom in a free nation is the freedom of private property, where citizens are free to buy, sell, own, use, rent, improve, hold, give (to a family member or friend or stranger), or donate (to a charitable organization) private property.

In the last few decades, especially during the Anti-Constitutional Era,[168] progressive socialists worked to limit many of our essential freedoms. Also, during that same period, the Constitution was repeatedly ignored and sidestepped by the Left.

In stark contrast to the Anti-Constitutional Era, in the new Conservative Era, our freedoms will again return.

More peace means we will see reduced external threats to our nation. Expect President Trump and Congress to follow through on promises to boost military spending and preparedness to protect America from any threat. Also, expect America to finally harden our electric grid system and establish a NORAD southern flank strategic posture to prevent a surprise electromagnetic pulse attack (EMP) from the south on America from North Korea or other nations.

Expect the threats from nations such as North Korea and Iran to subside as they recognize that America is once again a strong and resolute leader on the world stage.

In addition, terrorist threats will disappear as the ranks of terrorists are reduced overseas and their abilities to enter

America's homeland are systematically cutoff. Brutal gangs and drug lords will be barred from crossing our borders as well. Those gang members and drug lords already in the United States illegally will face certain deportation or jail time. With these changes, the risks of terrorist attacks, violence, and crime will all be substantially lowered in America's homeland.

More peace also means our neighborhoods and streets will be safer at night with reduced crime and drug use. Our police, firefighters, and other first responders will be safer as well.

More prosperity translates into a booming economy, with both GDP and the stock market growing at incredible rates. The economy seems to have taken off dramatically for the first time in about a decade.

Optimism indexes have risen. For example, the IBD/TIPP Economic Optimism Index in January 2018 is "signaling strong continued optimism" for the economy.[169]

U. S. manufacturing output is up as well. The fourth quarter 2017 manufacturing numbers are the best we have seen since 2010.[170]

GDP growth is about 3.2% in the third quarter of 2017 with some near-term forecasts of 4% and higher. That means Americans are feeling economically optimistic with more money in their checking accounts and in their 401Ks.

On the vital jobs front, the unemployment rate for December 2017, released in January 2018, is 4.1% on an overall downward trend since the election of President Trump. Unemployment has been hovering at numbers not seen in almost two decades.[171]

The technology, financial, and the energy sectors of our economy seemed to rally in early January 2018 as part of the stock boom that included the Dow Jones average breaking through the 26,000 milestone for the first time in its history.

As good as all these numbers have been in the early part of the new Conservative Era, more prosperity means the best is yet to come.

Expect the economy to continue to boom and to set and break more economic records during the new Conservative Era.

The rebirth of morality, freedom, peace, and prosperity means a plethora and blossoming of benefits that is a spin-off of the Conservative Enlightenment taking place as part of the new Conservative Era.

More Great News for America

There is more great news for America coming! My vision for America is enthusiastic, energetic, bright, and optimistic. Can you tell?

It is based on my study of American History, American politics, American presidents, the American economy, and importantly, the American people.

My vision for America is based on my research into American religious, cultural, political, economic, and dynamic electoral trends. That research includes long-range models that span from 24 to 36 years in length, short-range models that span 2 to 8 years in length, as well as dynamic electoral models and factors that span 1 to 24 months before a general election.

Some of the highlights of my vision are summarized below.

America is now in the early years of a new American Constitutional Era, the Conservative Era.

I think some polls are using questionable underlying models, adversely impacting their accuracy. Polls need to be studied, challenged, and questioned.

Both political parties will experience major political party realignments. The Republican Party will split in the next few years into two separate and distinct parties, the Conservative Party and the Republican Progressive Party. The Conservative Party will be the new majority party in America. The Republican Progressive Party will be the new minority party, taking the place of the

Democratic Party.

The Democratic Party's attempt to impeach President Trump will fail decisively. The Democratic Party will cease to exist as one of America's two major parties within a few years.

In the upcoming Congressional elections, the House will remain Republican with a loss of less than ten seats. It will become a more conservative body.

In the upcoming Congressional elections, the Senate Republicans will likely increase their majority control to 60 seats and will become filibuster-proof. The Senate will become more conservative as well.

In the upcoming 2020 presidential election, my early forecast is for President Trump to be reelected with an Electoral College win of greater than 350 Electoral Votes. In 2020, President Trump will also be the popular vote winner.

The Trump agenda will be substantially implemented during the course of his administration. President Trump will appoint three more Constitutional conservative justices to the Supreme Court. In fact, there will be a conservative super-majority of justices on the Supreme Court until the year 2050 or beyond, based on average appointment and retirement ages.

Along with the Conservative Era that has already started, I predict a new Conservative Enlightenment that will further strengthen, enhance, extend, and maintain our new Conservative Era for decades to come.

The new Conservative Enlightenment will include:

- The Return to Faith in God
- The Renaissance of Reason
- The Restoration of Education
- The Rebirth of Morality, Freedom, Peace, and Prosperity

The new Conservative Enlightenment will provide synergistic

benefits to develop and promote America's religious freedom, political freedom, and economic freedom, and will positively impact life in America on many different levels and in many different ways.

We will literally see the rebirth of morality in government and across America, a return to more individual freedom, peace with other nations and within America, and a level of prosperity greater than anything we have seen in America's stunning and remarkable history.

The Conservative Era is here. The new Conservative Enlightenment is coming.

There's More Great News for America coming!

America's future is fantastic!

Other Books by the Author

Great News for America

Renewing America and Its Heritage of Freedom

Choosing the Good Life

America's Economic War

About the Author

Gerard Francis Lameiro Ph.D. is an author, political analyst, and expert on forecast models. Dr. Lameiro is the author of five books and is a popular TV and Talk Radio show guest that does up to about 500 media interviews a year. Dr. Lameiro has been called by media hosts "America's #1 Political Analyst" and the "Nostradamus of Political Elections."

Dr. Lameiro accurately and consistently predicted a Trump victory long before most pollsters and pundits gave Trump even a small chance of winning the presidential election. Dr. Lameiro correctly predicted every State that candidate Trump actually carried in the 2016 election, including Florida, Pennsylvania, Ohio, Michigan, and Wisconsin.

Dr. Lameiro has worked on many political campaigns in various roles, including Ronald Reagan's 1976 and 1980 presidential election campaigns. Dr. Lameiro was a member of the 1980 Presidential Electoral College and personally cast one electoral vote for Ronald Reagan for President of the United States of America.

Notes

1) Gerard Francis Lameiro, *Great News for America* (Fort Collins, CO: Gerard Francis Lameiro, 2016).

2) Gerard Francis Lameiro, *Great News for America* (Fort Collins, CO: Gerard Francis Lameiro, 2016).

3) The White House, "A New National Security Strategy for a New Era," December 18, 2017, https://www.whitehouse.gov/articles/new-national-security-strategy-new-era/.

4) Jonathan Capehart, *The Washington Post*, ""Hands up, don't shoot" was built on a lie," March 16, 2015, https://www.washingtonpost.com/blogs/post-partisan/wp/2015/03/16/lesson-learned-from-the-shooting-of-michael-brown/?utm_term=.a35ca39ba266.

5) For an in-depth discussion of American Constitutional Eras in general and the new Conservative Era in particular, the reader is referred to my previous book: Gerard Francis Lameiro, *Great News for America* (Fort Collins, CO: Gerard Francis Lameiro, 2016).

6) Gerard Francis Lameiro, *Great News for America* (Fort Collins, CO: Gerard Francis Lameiro, 2016), pp. 145 – 148.

7) Gerard Francis Lameiro, *Great News for America* (Fort Collins, CO: Gerard Francis Lameiro, 2016), pp. 6 – 36.

8) United States Census Bureau, https://www.census.gov/.

9) Philip Bump, *The Atlantic Monthly Group,* "Here Is When Each Generation Begins and Ends, According to Facts," March 25, 2014, https://www.theatlantic.com/national/archive/2014/03/here-is-when-each-generation-begins-and-ends-according-to-facts/359589/.

10) Gary Langer, ABC News Internet Ventures, "2016 Race Stays at 47-43 Through Sunday (POLL)," November 7, 2016, http://abcnews.go.com/Politics/2016-race-stays-47-43-sunday-poll/story?id=43364234.

11) Gary Langer, ABC News Internet Ventures, "2016 Race Stays at 47-43 Through Sunday (POLL)," November 7, 2016, http://abcnews.go.com/Politics/2016-race-stays-47-43-sunday-poll/story?id=43364234.

12) Gary Langer, Gregory Holyk, Chad Kiewiet De Jonge, and Sofi Sinozich, ABC News Internet Ventures, "Clinton, Trump at Campaign's End: Still Close - and Still Unpopular (POLL)," November 7, 2016, http://abcnews.go.com/Politics/clinton-trump-campaigns-end-close-unpopular-poll/story?id=43344414.

13) IBD Staff, *Investor's Business Daily, Inc.,* "Clinton Vs. Trump: IBD/TIPP Presidential Election Tracking Poll," December 6, 2016, http://www.investors.com/politics/ibd-tipp-presidential-election-poll/.

14) IBD Staff, *Investor's Business Daily, Inc.,* "Clinton Vs. Trump: IBD/TIPP Presidential Election Tracking Poll," December 6, 2016, http://www.investors.com/politics/ibd-tipp-presidential-election-poll/.

15) Federal Election Commission, "OFFICIAL 2016 PRESIDENTIAL GENERAL ELECTION RESULTS: General Election Date: 11/08/2016," January 30, 2017, https://transition.fec.gov/pubrec/fe2016/2016presgeresults.pdf .

16) *Los Angeles Times,* "How the USC Dornsife/L.A. Times Daybreak tracking poll works," July 15, 2016, http://www.latimes.com/politics/la-na-pol-usc-daybreak-poll-methodology-20160714-snap-story.html.

17) *Los Angeles Times,* "How the USC Dornsife/L.A. Times Daybreak tracking poll works," July 15, 2016, http://www.latimes.com/politics/la-na-pol-usc-daybreak-poll-methodology-20160714-snap-story.html.

18) USC Dornsife/LA Times Presidential Election "Daybreak" Poll, "Understanding America Study," Note: no date of publication provided on webpage – copyright was listed as 2014, http://cesrusc.org/election/.

19) David Lauter, *Los Angeles Times,* "The USC/L.A. Times poll saw what other surveys missed: A wave of Trump support," November 8, 2016, http://www.latimes.com/politics/la-na-pol-usc-latimes-poll-20161108-story.html.

20) David Lauter, *Los Angeles Times,* "The USC/L.A. Times poll saw what other surveys missed: A wave of Trump support," November 8, 2016, http://www.latimes.com/politics/la-na-pol-usc-latimes-poll-20161108-story.html.

21) David Lauter, *Los Angeles Times,* "The USC/L.A. Times poll saw what other surveys missed: A wave of Trump support," November 8, 2016, http://www.latimes.com/politics/la-na-pol-usc-latimes-poll-20161108-story.html.

22) David Lauter, *Los Angeles Times,* "The USC/L.A. Times poll saw what other surveys missed: A wave of Trump support," November 8, 2016, http://www.latimes.com/politics/la-na-pol-usc-latimes-poll-20161108-story.html.

23) Herb Asher, *Polling and the Public: What Every Citizen Should Know, Ninth Edition* (Thousand Oaks, CA: CQ Press, an Imprint of

SAGE Publications, Inc., 2017), pp. 130 – 136.

24) Shane Goldmacher, Politico LLC, "America hits new landmark: 200 million registered voters," October 19, 2016, https://www.politico.com/story/2016/10/how-many-registered-voters-are-in-america-2016-229993.

25) Readers that want to study the process of polling in-depth can read any number of books and articles on the topic including the book by Erikson and Tedin: Robert S. Erikson and Kent L Tedin, *American Public Opinion: Ninth Edition* (London and New York, NY: Routledge, an Imprint of the Taylor & Francis Group, 2015), pp. 24 – 54.

26) Herbert F. Weisberg, Jon A. Krosnick, and Bruce D. Bowen, *An Introduction to Survey Research, Polling, and Data Analysis, Third Edition* (Thousand Oaks, CA: SAGE Publications, Inc., 1996).

27) Herb Asher, *Polling and the Public: What Every Citizen Should Know, Ninth Edition* (Thousand Oaks, CA: SAGE Publications, Inc., CQ Press, an Imprint of SAGE Publications, Inc., CQ Press is a registered trademark of Congressional Quarterly Inc., 2017).

28) Louis Nelson, Politico LLC, "Clinton leads Trump by 12 in new national poll," October 17, 2016, https://www.politico.com/story/2016/10/poll-who-is-winning-2016-229886.

29) ESPN Internet Ventures, "FiveThirtyEight: 2016 Election Forecast," November 8, 2016, https://projects.fivethirtyeight.com/2016-election-forecast/?ex_cid=2016-forecast-analysis.

30) Robert S. Erikson and Kent L Tedin, *American Public Opinion: Ninth Edition* (London and New York, NY: Routledge, an Imprint of the Taylor & Francis Group, 2015), pp. 30 – 32.

31) William E. Leuchtenburg, "Election of 1936," *History of American Presidential Elections 1789 – 2008, Fourth Edition, Volume II: 1872 – 1940,* Gil Troy, Arthur M. Schlesinger Jr. and Fred L. Israel, Editors (New York, NY: Facts On File, Inc., An Imprint of Infobase Learning, 2012), pp. 1057 – 1094.

32) Robert S. Erikson and Kent L Tedin, *American Public Opinion: Ninth Edition* (London and New York, NY: Routledge, an Imprint of the Taylor & Francis Group, 2015), pp. 30 – 32.

33) Gerard Francis Lameiro, *Great News for America* (Fort Collins, CO: Gerard Francis Lameiro, 2016), pp. 6 – 36.

34) Robert S. Erikson and Kent L Tedin, *American Public Opinion: Ninth Edition* (London and New York, NY: Routledge, an Imprint

of the Taylor & Francis Group, 2015), pp. 30 – 32.

35) "Case Study 2: The 1948 Presidential Election,"
https://www.math.upenn.edu/~deturck/m170/wk4/lecture/case2.ht
ml.

36) Richard S. Kirkendall, "Election of 1948," *History of American Presidential Elections 1789 – 2008, Fourth Edition, Volume III: 1944 – 2008,* Gil Troy, Arthur M. Schlesinger Jr. and Fred L. Israel, Editors (New York, NY: Facts On File, Inc., An Imprint of Infobase Learning, 2012), pp. 1157 – 1196.

37) Robert S. Erikson and Kent L Tedin, *American Public Opinion: Ninth Edition* (London and New York, NY: Routledge, an Imprint of the Taylor & Francis Group, 2015), pp. 30 – 32.

38) Robert S. Erikson and Kent L Tedin, *American Public Opinion: Ninth Edition* (London and New York, NY: Routledge, an Imprint of the Taylor & Francis Group, 2015), pp. 30 – 32.

39) Robert S. Erikson and Kent L Tedin, *American Public Opinion: Ninth Edition* (London and New York, NY: Routledge, an Imprint of the Taylor & Francis Group, 2015), pp. 30 – 32.

40) "Case Study 2: The 1948 Presidential Election,"
https://www.math.upenn.edu/~deturck/m170/wk4/lecture/case2.ht
ml.

41) "The 1948 Presidential Election Polls,"
http://www.randomservices.org/random/data/1948Election.html.

42) Andrew Mercer, Pew Research Center, "Oversampling is used to study small groups, not bias poll results," October 25, 2016,
http://www.pewresearch.org/fact-tank/2016/10/25/oversampling-is-used-to-study-small-groups-not-bias-poll-results/.

43) Andrew Mercer, Pew Research Center, "Oversampling is used to study small groups, not bias poll results," October 25, 2016,
http://www.pewresearch.org/fact-tank/2016/10/25/oversampling-is-used-to-study-small-groups-not-bias-poll-results/.

44) Andrew Mercer, Pew Research Center, "Oversampling is used to study small groups, not bias poll results," October 25, 2016,
http://www.pewresearch.org/fact-tank/2016/10/25/oversampling-is-used-to-study-small-groups-not-bias-poll-results/.

45) David Sherfinski, *The Washington Times, LLC,* "Rudy Giuliani: Polls are oversampling Democrats," October 25, 2016,
https://www.washingtontimes.com/news/2016/oct/25/rudy-giuliani-polls-are-oversampling-democrats/.

46) David Sherfinski, *The Washington Times, LLC,* "Rudy Giuliani: Polls are oversampling Democrats," October 25, 2016,
https://www.washingtontimes.com/news/2016/oct/25/rudy-giuliani-

polls-are-oversampling-democrats/.

47) Paul Bedard, *Washington Examiner,* "'Fraud': Mainstream polls use 29% more Democrats than Republicans," http://www.washingtonexaminer.com/fraud-mainstream-polls-use-29-more-democrats-than-republicans/article/2635271.

48) Paul Bedard, *Washington Examiner,* "'Fraud': Mainstream polls use 29% more Democrats than Republicans," http://www.washingtonexaminer.com/fraud-mainstream-polls-use-29-more-democrats-than-republicans/article/2635271.

49) Rasmussen Reports LLC, "Voters Don't Trust Media Fact-Checking," September 30, 2016, http://www.rasmussenreports.com/public_content/politics/general_p olitics/september_2016/voters_don_t_trust_media_fact_checking.

50) Jonathan Easley, CAPITOL HILL PUBLISHING CORP., A SUBSIDIARY OF NEWS COMMUNICATIONS, INC., "Poll: Majority says mainstream media publishes fake news," May 24, 2017, http://thehill.com/homenews/campaign/334897-poll-majority-says-mainstream-media-publishes-fake-news.

51) Harry Enten, FiveThirtyEight, "'Shy' Voters Probably Aren't Why The Polls Missed Trump," November 16, 2016, https://fivethirtyeight.com/features/shy-voters-probably-arent-why-the-polls-missed-trump/.

52) Sense About Science USA, "What the 2016 Presidential Election taught us about polling, predictions," November 15, 2016, http://senseaboutscienceusa.org/2016-presidential-election-taught-us-polling-predictions/. Quote was attributed in article to Rebecca Goldin, Ph.D., Director of STATS.org.

53) Pew Research Center, "Millennial and Gen X voter turnout increased in 2016…and among millennials, black turnout decreased," May 17, 2017, http://www.pewresearch.org/fact-tank/2017/05/12/black-voter-turnout-fell-in-2016-even-as-a-record-number-of-americans-cast-ballots/ft_17-05-12_voterturnout_millennialnew/.

54) *The New York Times Company,* "Presidential Election Results: Donald J. Trump Wins," August 9, 2017, https://www.nytimes.com/elections/results/president.

55) Kyle Cheney, POLITICO LLC, "Trump wins Electoral College vote," December 19, 2016, https://www.politico.com/story/2016/12/trump-electoral-college-win-democrats-infighting-232814.

56) Kyle Cheney, POLITICO LLC, "Trump wins Electoral College vote," December 19, 2016,

https://www.politico.com/story/2016/12/trump-electoral-college-win-democrats-infighting-232814.

57) Kyle Cheney, POLITICO LLC, "Trump wins Electoral College vote," December 19, 2016, https://www.politico.com/story/2016/12/trump-electoral-college-win-democrats-infighting-232814.

58) 270towin.com, "Split Electoral Votes in Maine and Nebraska," Note: no date of publication provided on webpage – copyright was listed as 2004-2017, https://www.270towin.com/content/split-electoral-votes-maine-and-nebraska/.

59) Gallup, "Party Affiliation," October 5-11, 2017, http://news.gallup.com/poll/15370/party-affiliation.aspx.

60) Gerard Francis Lameiro, Great News for America (Fort Collins, CO: Gerard Francis Lameiro, 2016), pp. 6 – 36.

61) Mark Hugo Lopez and Paul Taylor, Pew Research Center, "Latino Voters in the 2012 Election," November 7, 2012, http://www.pewhispanic.org/2012/11/07/latino-voters-in-the-2012-election/.

62) James Markarian, Forbes, "What The Election Taught Us About Predictive Analytics," February 8, 2017, https://www.forbes.com/sites/forbestechcouncil/2017/02/08/what-the-election-taught-us-about-predictive-analytics/#6151a67e6532.

63) Gerard Francis Lameiro, "American Constitutional Eras and Critical Presidential Elections," http://greatnewsforamerica.com/american-constitutional-eras/.

64) Emma Fierberg, Business Insider Inc., "A model that has correctly predicted the presidential election since 1980 says Clinton will have a landslide victory," November 1, 2016, http://www.businessinsider.com/moodys-analytics-predicts-hillary-clinton-win-presidential-election-2016-11.

65) Gerard Francis Lameiro, GreatNewsForAmerica.com, "Latest Electoral College Forecast: Trump 339 – Clinton 199 Electoral Votes," October 31, 2016, http://greatnewsforamerica.com/electoral-college-forecast/.

66) Jens Manuel Kroqstad and Mark Hugo Lopez, Pew Research Center, "Hillary Clinton won Latino vote but fell below 2012 support for Obama," November 29, 2016, http://www.pewresearch.org/fact-tank/2016/11/29/hillary-clinton-wins-latino-vote-but-falls-below-2012-support-for-obama/.

67) Gallup News, "Gallup Daily: Trump Job Approval," Viewed online on November 28, 2017, http://news.gallup.com/poll/201617/gallup-daily-trump-job-

approval.aspx.

68) Rasmussen Reports, LLC, "Daily Presidential Confidence Poll," November 28, 2017, http://www.rasmussenreports.com/public_content/politics/political_ updates/prez_track_nov28.

69) Sarah Dutton, Jennifer De Pinto, Fred Backus and Anthony Salvanto, CBS Interactive Inc., "CBS poll: Clinton's lead over Trump widens with three weeks to go," October 17, 2016, https://www.cbsnews.com/news/cbs-poll-clintons-lead-over-trump-widens-with-three-weeks-to-go/.

70) Florida Division of Elections, Florida Department of State, State of Florida, October 31, 2017, http://dos.myflorida.com/elections/data-statistics/voter-registration-statistics/voter-registration-monthly-reports/voter-registration-by-county-and-party/.

71) Florida Division of Elections, Florida Department of State, State of Florida, Viewed online on November 27, 2017, http://dos.myflorida.com/elections/data-statistics/voter-registration-statistics/voter-registration-monthly-reports/.

72) Florida Division of Elections, Florida Department of State, State of Florida, Viewed online on November 27, 2017, http://dos.myflorida.com/elections/data-statistics/voter-registration-statistics/voter-registration-monthly-reports/.

73) Gerard Francis Lameiro, *Great News for America* (Fort Collins, CO: Gerard Francis Lameiro, 2016), pp. 17 - 21.

74) Gilbert C. Fite, "Election of 1896," *History of American Presidential Elections 1789 – 2008, Fourth Edition, Volume II: 1872 – 1940,* Gil Troy, Arthur M. Schlesinger Jr. and Fred L. Israel, Editors (New York, NY: Facts On File, Inc., An Imprint of Infobase Learning, 2012), pp. 740 – 774.

75) Gilbert C. Fite, "Election of 1896," *History of American Presidential Elections 1789 – 2008, Fourth Edition, Volume II: 1872 – 1940,* Gil Troy, Arthur M. Schlesinger Jr. and Fred L. Israel, Editors (New York, NY: Facts On File, Inc., An Imprint of Infobase Learning, 2012), pp. 740 – 774.

76) Gerard Francis Lameiro, *Great News for America* (Fort Collins, CO: Gerard Francis Lameiro, 2016).

77) Nicholas Clairmont, The Big Think, Inc., "'Those Who Do Not Learn History Are Doomed To Repeat It.' Really?" Viewed on November 28, 2017, http://bigthink.com/the-proverbial-skeptic/those-who-do-not-learn-history-doomed-to-repeat-it-really.

78) Gerard Francis Lameiro, *Great News for America* (Fort Collins,

CO: Gerard Francis Lameiro, 2016).

79) Written by https://periodicpresidents.com/about/periodicpresidents/, The Periodic Table of the Presidents, "Which presidents were generals?" October 15, 2014, https://periodicpresidents.com/2014/10/15/which-presidents-were-generals/.

80) Written by https://periodicpresidents.com/about/periodicpresidents/, The Periodic Table of the Presidents, "Which presidents were generals?" October 15, 2014, https://periodicpresidents.com/2014/10/15/which-presidents-were-generals/.

81) Business Insider Inc., "11 quotes that show the great leadership of General George Patton," December 21, 2015, http://www.businessinsider.com/11-quotes-that-show-the-great-leadership-of-general-george-patton-2015-11/#1-a-pint-of-sweat-will-save-a-gallon-of-blood-1. Note: Original Article from Team Mighty, www.wearethemighty.com, Copyright 2015.

82) Rob Bluey, The Daily Signal, The Heritage Foundation, "New CNN Poll: 59% Oppose Obamacare," March 22, 2010, http://dailysignal.com/2010/03/22/new-cnn-poll-59-oppose-obamacare/.

83) Cable News Network, Turner Broadcasting System, Inc. CNN Library, "2015 Paris Terror Attacks Fast Facts," Updated October 31, 2017, http://www.cnn.com/2015/12/08/europe/2015-paris-terror-attacks-fast-facts/index.html.

84) Natalie Johnson, "California to Subsidize Health Care for Illegal Immigrant Children," *The Daily Signal,* dailysignal.com, June 19, 2015, http://dailysignal.com//2015/06/19/california-to-subsidize-healthcare-for-illegal-immigrant-children/ .

85) U.S. Electoral College Home, Office of the Federal Register, U.S. National Archives and Records Administration, "What are the Roles and Responsibilities of the Designated Parties in the Electoral College Process?" webpage was undated, https://www.archives.gov/federal-register/electoral-college/roles.html.

86) Gerard Francis Lameiro, "Ten Laws for Winning Presidential Elections," Copyrighted © 1992 – 2017, http://greatnewsforamerica.com/lameiros-ten-laws-for-winning-presidential-elections/.

87) Michael Patrick Leahy, Breitbart, "34 States Have Republican Governors, Most Since 1922," August 7, 2017, http://www.breitbart.com/big-government/2017/08/07/34-states-have-republican-governors-most-since-1922/.

88) Ballotpedia, The Lucy Burns Institute, "Governor of Alaska," Viewed online on December 2, 2017, https://ballotpedia.org/Governor_of_Alaska.

89) National Conference of State Legislatures, "State Partisan Composition," November 8, 2017, http://www.ncsl.org/research/about-state-legislatures/partisan-composition.aspx.

90) Nebraska Legislature, "History of the Nebraska Unicameral," Viewed online on December 2, 2017, http://nebraskalegislature.gov/about/history_unicameral.php.

91) Ballotpedia, The Lucy Burns Institute, "State government trifectas," Viewed online on December 2, 2017, https://ballotpedia.org/State_government_trifectas.

92) Ballotpedia, The Lucy Burns Institute, "State government trifectas," Viewed online on December 2, 2017, https://ballotpedia.org/State_government_trifectas.

93) Ballotpedia, The Lucy Burns Institute, "State government trifectas," Viewed online on December 2, 2017, https://ballotpedia.org/State_government_trifectas.

94) Michael Barone, National Review, "Yes, the Democrats, too, have big problems." September 23, 2016, http://www.nationalreview.com/article/440335/democratic-party-future-after-hillary-defeat.

95) Michael Barone, Washington Examiner, "Some free advice for the Democratic party," December 11, 2016, http://www.washingtonexaminer.com/some-free-advice-for-the-democratic-party/article/2609367.

96) Michael Barone, Washington Examiner, "Some free advice for the Democratic party," December 11, 2016, http://www.washingtonexaminer.com/some-free-advice-for-the-democratic-party/article/2609367.

97) Cressida Heyes, The Stanford Encyclopedia of Philosophy, The Metaphysics Research Lab, Center for the Study of Language and Information (CSLI), Stanford University, "Identity Politics," First published July 16, 2002; substantive revision March 23, 2016, Copyright 2016, https://plato.stanford.edu/entries/identity-politics/.

98) Mary Eberstadt, The Weekly Standard, "The Primal Scream of Identity Politics," October 27, 2017,

http://www.weeklystandard.com/the-primal-scream-of-identity-politics/article/2010234.

99) Stanley Greenberg and Page Gardner, The Hill, Capitol Hill Publishing Corp., A Subsidiary of News Communications, Inc., "The politics of the rising American electorate," December 5, 2016, http://thehill.com/blogs/pundits-blog/presidential-campaign/308804-the-politics-of-the-rising-american-electorate.

100) Michael Barone, Washington Examiner, "Some free advice for the Democratic party," December 11, 2016, http://www.washingtonexaminer.com/some-free-advice-for-the-democratic-party/article/2609367.

101) John Zogby, *We are Many, We are One: Neo-Tribes and Tribal Analytics in 21ˢᵗ Century America* (New Hartford, NY: John Zogby, 2016).

102) https://www.meetup.com/.

103) Shane Savitsky, Axios, "The media's Russia probe meltdown: 3 screw-ups in one week," December 8, 2017, https://www.axios.com/the-medias-russia-probe-meltdown-3-screw-ups-in-one-week-2515978886.html.

104) BBC, "Harvey Weinstein timeline: How the scandal unfolded," November 28, 2017, http://www.bbc.com/news/entertainment-arts-41594672.

105) Sophie Gilbert, TheAtlantic.com, The Atlantic Monthly Group, "The Movement of #MeToo," October 16, 2017, https://www.theatlantic.com/entertainment/archive/2017/10/the-movement-of-metoo/542979/.

106) 270towin.com, "1828 Presidential Election," Viewed online on December 12, 2017, https://www.270towin.com/1828_Election/.

107) Robert V. Remini, "Election of 1828," *History of American Presidential Elections 1789 – 2008, Fourth Edition, Volume I: 1789 – 1868,* Gil Troy, Arthur M. Schlesinger Jr. and Fred L. Israel, Editors (New York, NY: Facts On File, Inc., An Imprint of Infobase Learning, 2012), pp. 202 – 225.

108) Robert V. Remini, "Election of 1828," *History of American Presidential Elections 1789 – 2008, Fourth Edition, Volume I: 1789 – 1868,* Gil Troy, Arthur M. Schlesinger Jr. and Fred L. Israel, Editors (New York, NY: Facts On File, Inc., An Imprint of Infobase Learning, 2012), pp. 202 – 225.

109) Joel H. Silbey, "Election of 1836," *History of American Presidential Elections 1789 – 2008, Fourth Edition, Volume I: 1789 – 1868,* Gil Troy, Arthur M. Schlesinger Jr. and Fred L. Israel, Editors (New York, NY: Facts On File, Inc., An Imprint of Infobase

Learning, 2012), p. 254.

110) Roy F. Nichols and Philip S. Klein, "Election of 1856," *History of American Presidential Elections 1789 – 2008, Fourth Edition, Volume I: 1789 – 1868,* Gil Troy, Arthur M. Schlesinger Jr. and Fred L. Israel, Editors (New York, NY: Facts On File, Inc., An Imprint of Infobase Learning, 2012), pp. 437 – 464.

111) Roy F. Nichols and Philip S. Klein, "Election of 1856," *History of American Presidential Elections 1789 – 2008, Fourth Edition, Volume I: 1789 – 1868,* Gil Troy, Arthur M. Schlesinger Jr. and Fred L. Israel, Editors (New York, NY: Facts On File, Inc., An Imprint of Infobase Learning, 2012), pp. 437 – 464.

112) Dive and Discover (Registered Trademark of Woods Hole Oceanographic Institution), Woods Hole Oceanographic Institution, Copyright Date 2005, Viewed online on December 13, 2017, http://www.divediscover.whoi.edu/tectonics/tectonics-collide.html.

113) Bradford Richardson, *The Washington Times, LLC,* "Millennials would rather live in socialist or communist nation than under capitalism: Poll," November 4, 2017, https://www.washingtontimes.com/news/2017/nov/4/majority-millennials-want-live-socialist-fascist-o/.

114) Heather Long, CNN Money, Cable News Network, "The Obama economy in 10 charts," January 6, 2017, http://money.cnn.com/gallery/news/economy/2017/01/06/obama-economy-10-charts-final/3.html.

115) Adam Cancryn, POLITICO LLC, "Paul Krugman: Trump will bring global recession," November 9, 2016, https://www.politico.com/story/2016/11/krugman-trump-global-recession-2016-231055.

116) Bureau of Economic Analysis, U.S. Department of Commerce, "U.S. Economy at a Glance: Perspective from the BEA Accounts," Viewed online on January 4, 2018, https://www.bea.gov/newsreleases/glance.htm.

117) Patrick Gillespie and Chris Isidore, CNN Money, Cable News Network, "U.S. unemployment drops to lowest in 17 years," November 3, 2017, http://money.cnn.com/2017/11/03/news/economy/october-jobs-report/index.html.

118) Office of the Speaker, "Tax Cuts and Jobs Act," December 18, 2017, https://us13.campaign-archive.com/?u=5fb4099c8dedbe8a58e18dffb&id=92e8434769&e=78f8b98abd.

119) Office of the Speaker, "Tax Cuts and Jobs Act," December 18,

2017, https://us13.campaign-archive.com/?u=5fb4099c8dedbe8a58e18dffb&id=92e8434769&e=78f8b98abd.

120) Speaker Ryan Press Office, Office of the Speaker, "A Win for American Energy," December 14, 2017, https://www.speaker.gov/general/win-american-energy.

121) Clyde Wayne Crews, Competitive Enterprise Institute, "Ten Thousand Commandments 2017," May 31, 2017, https://cei.org/10kc2017 .

122) The White House, "President Trump Eliminates Job-Killing Regulations," March 30, 2017, https://www.whitehouse.gov/articles/president-trump-eliminates-job-killing-regulations/.

123) The White House, "President Trump Eliminates Job-Killing Regulations," March 30, 2017, https://www.whitehouse.gov/articles/president-trump-eliminates-job-killing-regulations/.

124) Philip A. Wallach and Nicholas W. Zeppos, The Brookings Institution, April 4, 2017, https://www.brookings.edu/research/how-powerful-is-the-congressional-review-act/.

125) The White House, "Presidential Executive Order on Reducing Regulation and Controlling Regulatory Costs," January 30, 2017, https://www.whitehouse.gov/presidential-actions/presidential-executive-order-reducing-regulation-controlling-regulatory-costs/.

126) The White House, "Press Briefing by Office of Information and Regulatory Affairs Administrator Neomi Rao on the Unified Agenda of Regulatory and Deregulatory Actions," December 14, 2017, https://www.whitehouse.gov/briefings-statements/press-briefing-office-information-regulatory-affairs-administrator-neomi-rao-unified-agenda-regulatory-deregulatory-actions/.

127) Matt O'Brien and Spencer Raley, Federation for American Immigration Reform, "The Fiscal Burden of Illegal Immigration on United States Taxpayers," September 27, 2017, https://fairus.org/issue/publications-resources/fiscal-burden-illegal-immigration-united-states-taxpayers.

128) Gerard Francis Lameiro, *Great News for America* (Fort Collins, CO: Gerard Francis Lameiro, 2016), pp. 48 – 50.

129) U. S. Citizenship and Immigration Services, "Green Card Through the Diversity Immigrant Visa Program," Last Reviewed/Updated: November 27, 2017, https://www.uscis.gov/greencard/diversity-visa.

130) A Notice by the State Department, Federal Register, The Daily Journal of the United States Government, "Bureau of Consular Affairs; Registration for the Diversity Immigrant (DV-2019) Visa Program," Document Citation: 82 FR 48563, Page: 48563-48571 (9 pages), Agency/Docket Number: Public Notice: 10174, Document Number: 2017-22638, October 18, 2017, https://www.federalregister.gov/documents/2017/10/18/2017-22638/bureau-of-consular-affairs-registration-for-the-diversity-immigrant-dv-2019-visa-program.

131) NumbersUSA Action, "End Chain Immigration," Viewed online on January 5, 2017, https://www.numbersusa.com/solutions/end-chain-migration.

132) NumbersUSA Action, "End Chain Immigration," Viewed online on January 5, 2017, https://www.numbersusa.com/solutions/end-chain-migration.

133) NumbersUSA Action, "End Chain Immigration," Viewed online on January 5, 2017, https://www.numbersusa.com/solutions/end-chain-migration.

134) Mark Krikorian, National Review, "DACA, DACA, Bo-Baca . . . The prospects of an amnesty deal are fading," January 8, 2018, http://www.nationalreview.com/article/455169/donald-trump-daca-deal-prospects-fade.

135) LawLogix, Hyland Software, Inc., "What Is the DREAM Act and Who are DREAMers?" July 29, 2013, https://www.lawlogix.com/what-is-the-dream-act-and-who-are-dreamers/.

136) LawLogix, Hyland Software, Inc., "What Is the DREAM Act and Who are DREAMers?" July 29, 2013, https://www.lawlogix.com/what-is-the-dream-act-and-who-are-dreamers/.

137) Mark Krikorian, National Review, "DACA, DACA, Bo-Baca . . . The prospects of an amnesty deal are fading," January 8, 2018, http://www.nationalreview.com/article/455169/donald-trump-daca-deal-prospects-fade.

138) Laura Meckler, *The Wall Street Journal,* "Trump Administration Seeks $18 Billion Over Decade to Expand Border Wall," January 5, 2018, https://www.wsj.com/articles/trump-administration-seeks-18-billion-over-decade-to-expand-border-wall-1515148381.

139) Laura Meckler, *The Wall Street Journal,* "Trump Administration Seeks $18 Billion Over Decade to Expand Border

Wall," January 5, 2018, https://www.wsj.com/articles/trump-administration-seeks-18-billion-over-decade-to-expand-border-wall-1515148381.

140) Jasmine C. Lee, Rudy Omri, and Julia Preston, *The New York Times,* "What Are Sanctuary Cities?" February 6, 2017, https://www.nytimes.com/interactive/2016/09/02/us/sanctuary-cities.html.

141) Bryan Griffith and Jessica Vaughan, Center for Immigration Studies, "Maps: Sanctuary Cities, Counties, and States," July 27, 2017, https://cis.org/Map-Sanctuary-Cities-Counties-and-States.

142) Matthew Rozsa, Salon Media Group, Inc., "A blue wave in 2018? Experts say Doug Jones' win is a very bad sign for the GOP," December 13, 2017, https://www.salon.com/2017/12/13/a-blue-wave-in-2018-experts-say-doug-jones-win-is-a-very-bad-sign-for-the-gop/.

143) Ballotpedia, "Minnesota's 8th Congressional District election, 2016," Viewed online on January 11, 2018, https://ballotpedia.org/Minnesota%27s_8th_Congressional_District_election,_2016.

144) Sabato's Crystal Ball, University of Virginia Center for Politics, The Rector and Visitors of the University of Virginia, "2018 House," January 10, 2018, http://www.centerforpolitics.org/crystalball/2018-house/.

145) Gerard Francis Lameiro, *Great News for America* (Fort Collins, CO: Gerard Francis Lameiro, 2016).

146) Bradford Richardson, *The Washington Times, LLC,* "Millennials would rather live in socialist or communist nation than under capitalism: Poll," November 4, 2017, https://www.washingtontimes.com/news/2017/nov/4/majority-millennials-want-live-socialist-fascist-o/.

147) News Release, Bureau of Labor Statistics, U. S. Department of Labor, "The Employment Situation — December 2017," USDL-18-0024, January 5, 2018, https://www.bls.gov/news.release/pdf/empsit.pdf.

148) Everett Rosenfeld, CNBC, "Trump launches attack on Syria with 59 Tomahawk missiles," April 7, 2017, https://www.cnbc.com/2017/04/06/us-military-has-launched-more-50-than-missiles-aimed-at-syria-nbc-news.html.

149) The President, The White House, "Statement by President Donald J. Trump on the Defeat of ISIS in Raqqah," October 21, 2017, https://www.whitehouse.gov/briefings-statements/statement-president-donald-j-trump-defeat-isis-raqqah/.

150) FoxNews.com, "Purported ISIS warning claims terror cells in

place in 15 states," FoxNews.com, May 6, 2015, http://www.foxnews.com/us/2015/05/06/purported-isis-warning-claims-terror-cells-in-place-in-15-states/ .

151) Franz-Stefan Gady, The Diplomat, "3 US Carrier Strike Groups Hold Massive Naval Drill with South Korean, Japanese Navies in Western Pacific," November 13, 2017, https://thediplomat.com/2017/11/3-us-carrier-strike-groups-hold-massive-naval-drill-with-south-korean-japanese-navies-in-western-pacific/.

152) Natalie Schachar, *Los Angeles Times,* "Oklahoma's Ten Commandments case is part of an age-old battle in U.S.," July 9, 2015, http://www.latimes.com/nation/la-na-ten-commandments-20150709-story.html.

153) Morgan Lee, *Christianity Today,* "Mt. Soledad Cross Controversy Ends after 25 Years," July 22, 2015, http://www.christianitytoday.com/news/2015/july/mt-soledad-cross-controversy-ends-veterans-memorial.html.

154) If you want to read more about God, freedom, and politics, please consider reading two of my previous books: *Renewing America and Its Heritage of Freedom,* and *America's Economic War.*

155) Gerard Francis Lameiro, *Great News for America* (Fort Collins, CO: Gerard Francis Lameiro, 2016).

156) Matthew Green, KQED News, KQED Inc., "MAP: States Where Convicted Felons Can't Vote," November 4, 2016, http://ww2.kqed.org/lowdown/2016/11/04/map-felon-voter-disenfranchisement-by-the-numbers/.

157) Matthew Green, KQED News, KQED Inc., "MAP: States Where Convicted Felons Can't Vote," November 4, 2016, http://ww2.kqed.org/lowdown/2016/11/04/map-felon-voter-disenfranchisement-by-the-numbers/.

158) Matthew Green, KQED News, KQED Inc., "MAP: States Where Convicted Felons Can't Vote," November 4, 2016, http://ww2.kqed.org/lowdown/2016/11/04/map-felon-voter-disenfranchisement-by-the-numbers/.

159) John Fund, National Review, "The World Requires Voter ID, but George Soros and Hillary Clinton Are Determined the U.S. Won't," July 16, 2015, http://www.nationalreview.com/article/421292/voter-id-other-countries-require.

160) Politico LLC, "2016 Presidential Election Results," December 13, 2016, https://www.politico.com/mapdata-2016/2016-election/results/map/president/.

161) Rowan Scarborough, *The Washington Times,* "More than 5,000 out-of-state voters may have tipped New Hampshire against Trump," September 7, 2017, https://www.washingtontimes.com/news/2017/sep/7/voter-fraud-alert-over-5000-new-hampshire-presiden/.

162) Rowan Scarborough, *The Washington Times,* "More than 5,000 out-of-state voters may have tipped New Hampshire against Trump," September 7, 2017, https://www.washingtontimes.com/news/2017/sep/7/voter-fraud-alert-over-5000-new-hampshire-presiden/..

163) Rowan Scarborough, *The Washington Times,* "More than 5,000 out-of-state voters may have tipped New Hampshire against Trump," September 7, 2017, https://www.washingtontimes.com/news/2017/sep/7/voter-fraud-alert-over-5000-new-hampshire-presiden/.

164) Politico LLC, "2016 Presidential Election Results," December 13, 2016, https://www.politico.com/mapdata-2016/2016-election/results/map/president/.

165) Gerard Francis Lameiro, *Renewing America and Its Heritage of Freedom: What Freedom-Loving Americans Can Do to Help* (Fort Collins, CO: Gerard Francis Lameiro, 2014).

166) Gerard Francis Lameiro, *Renewing America and Its Heritage of Freedom: What Freedom-Loving Americans Can Do to Help* (Fort Collins, CO: Gerard Francis Lameiro, 2014).

167) Gerard Francis Lameiro, *Renewing America and Its Heritage of Freedom: What Freedom-Loving Americans Can Do to Help* (Fort Collins, CO: Gerard Francis Lameiro, 2014), p. 277.

168) Gerard Francis Lameiro, *Great News for America* (Fort Collins, CO: Gerard Francis Lameiro, 2016), pp. 29 – 35.

169) IBD Staff, *Investor's Business Daily,* "IBD/TIPP Poll: Economic Optimism Index," Viewed online on January 17, 2018, https://www.investors.com/news/economy/ibdtipp-poll-economic-optimism-index/.

170) Katia Dmitrieva, Bloomberg, "U.S. Manufacturing Output Rose in December for Fourth Month," January 17, 2018, https://www.bloomberg.com/news/articles/2018-01-17/u-s-manufacturing-output-rose-in-december-for-a-fourth-month.

171) Patrick Gillespie and Chris Isidore, CNN Money, Cable News Network, "U.S. unemployment drops to lowest in 17 years," November 3, 2017, http://money.cnn.com/2017/11/03/news/economy/october-jobs-report/index.html.

CPSIA information can be obtained
at www.ICGtesting.com
Printed in the USA
LVOW10s1716220318
570811LV00013B/995/P